# WE TEACH THEM ALL

## Teachers Writing About Diversity

### June Kuzmeskus

*editor for the Massachusetts Field Center*
*for Teaching and Learning*

Stenhouse Publishers
York, Maine

To all the teachers who struggle to write – may their voices be heard.

Stenhouse Publishers, 226 York Street, York, Maine 03909

Copyright © 1996 The Massachusetts Field Center for Teaching and Learning

All royalty earnings from the sale of this book will help support the Massachusetts Field Center for Teaching and Learning's writing programs for teachers.

"I.M.O.B." and "The Principal Makes an Exception to the No Hat Rule," by E. J. Miller Laino previously appeared in *Negative Capability*.

Library of Congress Cataloging-in-Publication Data

We teach them all : teachers writing about diversity / June Kuzmeskus, editor for the Massachusetts Field Center for Teaching and Learning.
    p.    cm.
    ISBN 1-57110-032-6 (alk. paper)
    1. Teachers in literature.   2. Teachers—Massachusetts.
3. Pluralism (Social sciences)—Massachusetts.   I. Kuzmeskus, June.
II. Massachusetts Field Center for Teaching and Learning.
LB1785.W4   1996
371.1'009744—dc20                                                     95-50951
                                                                              CIP

Cover and interior design by Darci Mehall

Typeset by Achorn Graphics

Manufactured in the United States of America on acid-free paper

99 98 97 96 8 7 6 5 4 3 2 1

# CONTENTS

# Contents

# FOREWORD

We have all seen the headlines: "Broad Growth Is Found in U.S. Hispanic, Asian Populations." "Gap Between Rich and Poor Grows Wider." "Hispanic Population Outnumbers Blacks in Four Major Cities as Demographics Shift." "Parents Call Role Tougher in '90s Than in the Past." "Many of Youngest Face Hurdle of Poverty."

These are the facts of life in the United States at the end of the twentieth century. We are becoming an ever more multifaceted society, socially and demographically. Growing numbers of children grow up in poverty, in racially isolated communities, with less contact with fewer adults. The number of immigrant students enrolled in public schools is on the increase. More children with distinct learning needs press our teachers for their attention.

But the headlines invite different interpretations and elicit different responses, depending on the reader. Some read the headlines as small-craft warnings and join in calls to batten down the hatches, reef the sails, and retreat to familiar ports. Amid the choppy seas and high winds of change, the fearful seek the safe shores of traditional schools and press to secure a conformity of behavior and student performance. Frightened for their future, the anxious cast about for a place where those who do not fit a particular image of what students should be remain conveniently invisible.

Others read the same headlines as travel advisories that alert us to the challenges of a journey into new territory. Looking ahead, the well-prepared prescribe and initiate plans suited to the demands of the passage. These travelers, with guidebooks to multicultural curriculum, mainstreaming, integration, and bilingual education can look to the future with more anticipation than trepidation. Yet although these tools may be necessary, they alone are not sufficient for the rigors of the journey.

The teachers whose insights and epiphanies illuminate this volume are among the best-prepared for the journey ahead. It is not that they do not feel the anxiety of change. Indeed, their stories, poems, essays, and reflections bear witness to the fact that as we undertake the challenges of more diverse classrooms, we cannot avoid the worries of the traveler, no matter how well prepared we are. As they lay out their fears—of making mistakes, of seeming foolish, and especially of failing to connect with the children before them—these teachers reveal that they are far from confident that they are up to the task before them.

But in describing their trials and errors, successes and failures with particular students, these teachers tell us something even more important: Beyond the right tools or latest techniques, the teaching of diverse students requires uncommon courage and a firm resolve to look clearly at each child within the context of his or her circumstances, despite whatever emotions—exhilaration, shock, rage, despair—such encounters may summon up.

Why do these teachers decide to experience what would be so easy to avoid, to see what would be so easy to ignore? What is it that compels them to let down the veil of labels, stereotypes, or rationalizations that protects so many of us from seeing each student as unique and whole? What beliefs must these teachers draw from to explore and discover each student's strengths and make those manifest for others to see?

Above all, this book reminds us of a simple fact: If you can't reach 'em, you can't teach 'em. As our classrooms change, acknowledging differences and affirming the richness and complexity of diverse classrooms requires not just new skills and knowledge, but renewed convictions about the rewards of human connection.

The teachers whose works are included here make these rewards obvious. Their writings show us that encounters with diverse students, with challenging students, can enlarge our world beyond the narrowness of place or personal experience. We too can choose to make the connections that open doors to the deepest and broadest stuff of human experience. These teachers tell us that if we let them, our students will make us global citizens, even if we never leave home. They remind us that to create classrooms where students are safe to be themselves is to build schools where we are safe to be ourselves as well. And if we persist, we can obtain the best rewards of all: the gift of our students' stories and what they reveal not only about their lives, but about our own.

ANNE WHEELOCK

# INTRODUCTION

This book is filled with writings by teachers about their lives and those of their students. Nearly all the contributors have been supported in their writing by the Massachusetts Field Center for Teaching and Learning, through their attendance at an annual retreat, "Teachers' Voices: Reflecting, Writing, and Sharing." This event is prompted by a belief in the inextricable connections between writing and thinking and, consequently, the assumption that writing is a powerful tool for learning.

The first such retreat took place in 1987, when twenty-four participants spent two days away from their schools and families at a serene and beautiful site, interacting in ways that promoted their reflection and writing. Over the years, though the sites have changed, the number of participants has risen to sixty, and the length of time has increased to three days, the initial vision and components of the writers' retreats have remained the same.

In the belief that to teach writing well, one must be a writer and experience the writer's array of mental activities—insecurity, inspiration, frustration, discipline, joy of expression—the Field Center created a structure and an environment that nurtures creativity and affirms the value of each participant's writing, the contribution each can make to professional dialogue. How that is accomplished is detailed in the last section, "Organizing and Conducting a Writers' Retreat for Teachers."

Recognizing that teachers are an often overlooked source of knowledge about education, the Field Center has created a variety of opportunities for teachers to reflect and write about their practice and for their voices to be heard by both peers and policymakers. To that end, the Center conducts forums and conferences, including the writers' retreats; administers mini-grant programs; publishes books, booklets, and a bimonthly newsletter, distributed to over seven thousand educators, that features writing by teachers; and runs an annual writers' contest.

This collection of stories, poems, and personal essays is a gleaning of writing that has emerged from the Field Center's forums for teacher writing, primarily the writers' retreats. Much of that writing is drawn from the teachers' personal lives and intimate relationships beyond the school walls. For this volume, however, the final cut was limited to pieces related to the theme of diversity in the classroom, a theme that is compelling and pertinent to all educators.

At the beginning and end of each section the authors reflect on the source, context, and significance of their pieces.

The first section, "Where We Meet," looks at life in school. To know life in today's schools is to recognize the extent of the gulf between the experience and consciousness of most teachers and those of many of their students. Those who bridge that gulf find and nurture the kinship that is often a prerequisite of learning.

The following section, "Who We Are," hints at the varied identities behind the hostile and hopeful faces in the halls of our schools. Clearly, the contributors to this volume have answered their students' need for empathy, or at least their need to be seen and heard. Along with portraits of the students is the conscious, purposeful inclusion of the teachers themselves as part of the learning community.

To fully appreciate "What We Learn," as described in the section of that name, the reader must leap beyond the conventional boundaries of content and subject area to examine the less acknowledged body of knowledge that makes up so much of the reality of school life and so forms students' learning. No doubt the writers of this book remember all those times they were admonished by their own teachers with the words, "In order to learn, you must listen," for what they show us is that when teachers really listen to their students, everyone learns the most astounding things.

The section "What We Bring" gets to the heart of how significant persons in the lives of students, including their teachers, intervene in their learning. What surrounds, identifies, touches, and motivates students is more powerful than all the enrichment or remedial courses in the world. Seeing those forces, building from that knowledge, creating the bridge needed for students to get from here to there is where real teaching and learning begin.

Although we did not sit down together in the same room at the same time, consider the section "Acknowledging and Supporting the Diversity of All Learners" a sort of conversation among the contributors in which they discuss the knowledge, beliefs, understandings, skills, and practices they find most helpful in creating classrooms that support diversity.

The last section, "Organizing and Conducting a Writers' Retreat for Teachers," is a detailed description of the Field Center's writing retreats. With the information about how the people, program, and location work together is the rationale that underpins the retreat and provides cohesion between this annual event and the other opportunities for learning, growth, and leadership sponsored by the Field Center.

The appendix contains a sample plan for a writing group session. Facilitators' plans vary according to each individual's own notion of what is most effective and suitable. This plan is included as just one possible approach.

# I

## Where We Meet

We meet in the halls, the classroom, the gym, the cafeteria, the school yard. We meet at lunch, in detention, to learn, to teach. For several hours, five days a week, we are each other's city or town, family or community.

How do we see ourselves? How do we see each other?

LINDA FERNSTEN: *There are so many experiences we share as teachers that we don't get a chance to discuss. I dare say many teachers know [the] Desk Hangers they'll read about in this section: they may not have had a name for them before, but they will recognize them.*

How does the outside world see us? In Ruth Weiner's piece, "Yesterday Meets Tomorrow," two wary senior citizens tiptoe down a school corridor, waiting to be mugged at every turn.

How are we related?

DIANE DANTHONY: *The group of students in "The Hardest Class Ever" is gone, but their shadow lingers. There were only eight, but they filled the room . . . with sudden joyful outbursts, unexplained brawls, stony silences, angry frustrations with the demands of school, sadnesses about something that happened last period or yesterday or long ago.*

# THE HARDEST CLASS EVER

*diane danthony*

One bloodies her knuckles
on the bulletin board.
Faint reddish lines remain
to trace her anger.

One whose father has died
slips in unnoticed.
A shimmering silver thread binds her ankles.
She looks down when my eyes reach her.
We have forgotten the sound of her voice.

Another is bent
over a tiny, palm held mirror.
She wears a colorful shell
with fine brittle lines
scarring the surface.
A carefully guarded ceramic egg.

One is new to this class.
Wistful sky and ocean poems
penciled in a ragged journal.
She runs away that weekend.
We do not see her again.

The one who sits alone was a dancer.
She buries her head in her arms,
dark hair spilling over the desk.
Black Chinese shoes, worn thin,
hold the memory of an earlier life.

One stretches himself into the doorway.
Arms and legs strung tight,
against the bright hall.
A pale starfish,
he grips the four corners of the jamb
and leans toward laughter from the next room.

The sister of another has broken her neck.
She is now the older sister.
She kisses her papers,
the mirror in the girls' room,
polished cinderblock hallways.
Her lipstick signature fades by daylight.

One has moments separate from us.
He stands at attention, a nod,
a whisper.
Alone with the voices we cannot hear.

There is no looking away.
I have opened my heart
and I am waiting.

# YESTERDAY MEETS TOMORROW

*Ruth E. Weiner*

Frank aimed his remote and flipped channels.

"Hey, Mabel!" he shouted. "Cable says the high school has a free lunch for senior citizens today. Whaddaya say we go?"

"High school? Isn't that where kids roam with machetes and hand grenades?"

"A free lunch, Mabel! Let's take our chances."

Mabel left her purse at home. Frank hitched suspenders to his pants and put on his new running shoes.

Together they entered the building. Two students greeted them. One had a shaved head, except for her two floppy ponytails above tri-earringed ears; the other wore his hat backwards and his pants drooped below his boxer shorts.

"Welcome to Major High," they said as a third student, with cut-off gloves and black fingernails, handed them visitors' badges and a map of the school. "Follow the arrows to the cafeteria, or just amble around the building if you'd like. You're welcome to drop in on any classes on your way through."

Mouthing thank yous, Frank and Mabel clutched each other's hand and tiptoed down the quiet corridor until they heard Greek music coming from one of the rooms.

They popped their heads into the classroom, where they saw two dozen students in two concentric circles, holding hands and moving four steps left, four steps right, then into the center and out with a whoop. On the board and walls were Greek symbols, large maps of Greece, and posters of gods and goddesses; on the desks stood handmade replicas of buildings and statues. Everywhere Frank and Mabel looked, things looked Greek to them.

They relaxed a bit as they continued down the corridor until they saw a young man dressed in cowboy boots and hat standing outside a classroom.

"Young man," demanded Mabel in her best teacher-like voice, "why are you standing here?"

"We're in the middle of a mock trial. See, look inside. Mr. Conrad, in the black robe, is the judge and those twelve over there are the jury. I'm Slim from *Of Mice and Men* and I'm going to get George Milton, the defendant, off the hook—if I can. Ah, there's my name being called. Wish me luck."

Just then, Frank and Mabel heard a commotion further down the hall. Mabel jumped and Frank was ready to turn around, but as they approached the classroom, they realized that students were just rearranging their desks into small groups, then settling in to read their papers to each other.

Frank and Mabel sauntered to the cafeteria. Along the way a bulletin board caught their eye: Vote Today on the Adoption of the School Constitution! Sign up for Project Volunteer with Mr. Tate in D210. The Recycling Committee Meets Wednesday in B110 with Mrs. Barry. Support Your School: Buy a T-shirt!

Inside the cafeteria, they noticed students distributing the school newspaper, students dressed in Disney costumes selling tickets for the school play, students chatting with each other, with teachers, with senior citizens like themselves.

They looked again at the map they had received. The computer labs were on the third floor—they wondered if they could try them. The library was near the office—they wondered if they could take out a book. The gym was next to the cafeteria—they wondered if they could play shuffleboard.

"Let's buy a T-shirt, Frank."

"Let's eat first," he replied as he bellied up to the lunch line next to a tall boy with a skeleton earring and spiked rainbow hair. "I like it here," said Frank. "How about we bring the grandkids with us next time?"

# BACKING OFF

*Beverly C. Lucey*

The boys were hanging around the front of the high school during the first part of August. Even though they'd still be attending the middle school as seventh graders in less than a month, secretly at least two of them were hoping the dull, sullen students making up courses in summer school would think they might be freshmen or even sophomores. Jason was getting tall and had begun smoking, so hey! they looked pretty cool. Ronny was wearing a faded Guns 'n' Roses T-shirt that he'd lifted from Pedro their skinny Fresh Air Kid, the day Pedro had left for his home in the Bronx. Definitely cool. Mike (who preferred to be called M-16) had talked his brother into taking him to get a haircut in a nearby college town where they knew how to do way cooler stuff than this boonie place. Mike secretly hoped to become known as The White Wrapper of New England. He wrote this name on all his notebooks last year. Spelling was not his strong point, but he devoted hours a day to responding to any request in rhyme. ("Yo. You askin' me to go down town / but that ain't the way it's goin' down / I ain't goin' to no grocery store / 'Cause I don't want to eat at home no more. Huh.") He was cool in his own way, the guys decided. The three of them had been friends forever—since fifth grade. But summer was starting to get on their nerves. Older guys cruised by in their hot cars, blaring music and making deals, getting the pretty blonds and the hot-looking redheads.

Still, for Jason, Ronny, and Mike there was nothing to do. Skateboarding off the curb was not impressing the summer school girls. Ronny's knees were a scabby mess from trying to coast through the drained pool near the tracks. He kept saying he was "gleaming the cube" after renting that video every dollar night for five weeks. The town had run out of money to fill the municipal pool this year, and being twelve was about as nowhere a time as this place felt.

But this steaming boredom scene evaporated five minutes later when that big guy, Natie Graves's crazy older brother, skimmed up to the curb in a shiny Trans Am offering them action and a beeper. All of a sudden twelve years old seemed just perfect, like television with no commercial breaks. No way they could get caught, Mike assured them all. Jason echoed Mike. But Ronny, holding his skateboard like a teddy bear, looked at Buzzy Graves behind the wheel in front of him, smiling like the devil, and backed away, back into childhood for maybe just another day.

# THE PRINCIPAL MAKES AN EXCEPTION TO THE NO HAT RULE

*E. J. Miller Laino*

The principal says
their hats may look harmless,
mostly baseball caps with team logos
but they are a breeding ground for trouble.
Kids who wear hats
with the emblem of the California Angels
could become a suburban gang,
call themselves the Crazy Angels,
hang out at McDonalds,
smoke cigarettes, pot, have sex.
Kids need to understand
that we, without hats, mean business.
Without hats *they* could become
computer whizzes, merit scholars, cooperative
youngsters who know the magic words
please and thank you.
Everyone knows how kids hide
under hats, brain cells
popping like corn, kids popping Lifesavers,
popping pills in the bathroom;
who really knows what's cooking
inside the heads of those hat wearers,
those rule breakers?
Then she comes back to school.
comes back with a face so white,
porcelain dolls ask to be repainted.
Her still blue eyes plead
*remember me.* Hatless
boys and girls stand silently and watch
her slow progress down the corridor,
but it's the Notre Dame hat, navy blue,

gold rim, that shouts.
The principal includes this in the daily bulletin:
*There will be one female student*
*wearing a hat. She's had a long series of medical treatments. No*
*other student*
*has permission to wear a hat.* Repeat.
No other students may wear hats.

# RATANA'S STORY

*Diana Callahan*

It was the first day of school—new clothes, new backpack, new class, new teacher, new language, new country. The last time I had been in school was in Thailand. I only went for a short time after our family fled our home in Cambodia. I think we've always been leaving Cambodia—my name actually means "Little Runaway"; at least, that's what my older cousins, giggling, told the teacher shortly after that first day. In any case, I entered school in America as a first grader despite the fact that I am nine years old. I had never been to school before, and the school in the camp had been considered a kindergarten.

Those first few days were unbearable. The teacher always seemed angry—shaking her finger and yelling at me to stop struggling with the other boys. No adult in Cambodia or the camps ever insisted on peaceful acceptance of another child's pushing you or getting ahead of you. Everything there had been a fight—fight for food, fight for position, fight for rights. My ability to fight only seemed to upset this teacher. Although I couldn't understand their words, I knew the other children were constantly complaining about my ability to dominate them, and the teacher was committed to intervening in behalf of those weaker and less deserving than myself.

In the class, there was another boy from Cambodia, but he was weak and refused to talk to me in the language I knew we shared. When I pleaded with him to set the teacher straight, he would only frown and turn away, pretending he did not hear or understand.

I enjoyed the paper and pencils the teacher gave me. The other children always began immediately and boldly. I took this task very seriously and carefully sketched the letters of my name, which my uncle had taught me, and the faces I remembered from home. I used the paper and pencil as I had seen adults use them in Cambodia, with quick, light strokes and angular, precise lines. Although I liked to draw, my favorite time of the day was when we did math with the brightly colored shapes that were stored in the blue plastic tubs. I liked making patterns and understood what I was expected to do with the shapes and colors. When we finished, I knew everything had to be put away, so I worked hard and got the attention of the teacher. Now she didn't wag her finger at me and make unpleasant faces. She nodded and smiled, and the other children pitched in to help me.

Recess was a good time, too. I could run freely and often got a chance to kick the soccer ball that seemed to be in constant motion on the playground. The other children often shared the food they brought from home. Strange American food! But it was good. One day I tasted the "Fruit Roll-Ups" that everyone seemed to be enjoying. The children laughed when I spit out the gummy thing and said "Bad! Taste bad!" Even the teacher laughed.

Monday morning always began with the other children talking about their weekends at home and then drawing and writing about them in a news story. Everyone would read to the teacher, and she would add American print under their letters. She always added American words about my picture, too. Soon I began to use the words I had memorized from the wall at the front of the room to add American print to my picture. My stories were always so little. I wrote things like "I like apple"; "I go store." I had so much more to say but didn't even know the words to speak! Some of the other children began helping me. They would tell me the American words about my pictures. They liked the detailed pictures I drew about a land they never knew. The teacher liked my pictures, too. I often gave her my drawings and learned to inscribe them with her name and the word "to." She put every one of those pictures on her closet door or on the wall by her desk. The whole space was covered with them!

The teacher had always tried to get John, the other Cambodian boy, to talk to me. Sometimes he would answer me with one word or give in to the teacher's pleading to translate directions or answers to my questions. One day the class was discussing pets. The teacher persuaded John to ask me if I had a dog in Cambodia. A wonderful thing happened! John asked me the other children's questions in Cambodian and translated my answers. Everyone was excited to learn something about my life in Cambodia. They all listened to me. I think the other children finally saw me as a boy just like themselves instead of a stranger that didn't know or understand anything. The teacher moved our seats next to each other. Now John and I often chatted in Cambodian during the day. He answered many of my questions, and we began to learn together.

On Thursday afternoon, the fourth graders came to our class to read. There were four Cambodian students in that class. The teacher always made sure one of them was my partner. I liked working with them. They would read to me in English, but they would tell me the story and answer my questions in Cambodian. I began working with them early in the morning before school started. They would take turns. The teacher would give us the story we would read in class that day. The fourth grader would read it to me and we would talk about it. That way, when it came time to read in class, I knew the story so I could say many of the American words.

The teacher always read lots of stories to us. She was reading a different version of "The Three Little Pigs" to us when I noticed the stick house that the second little pig had built. It was exactly like my home in Cambodia—raised high above the ground on stilt-like legs. I pointed and began shouting, "Like Cambodia house!" The teacher knew exactly what I meant. Her entire wall was covered with pictures of that house! She stopped reading and we all discussed the picture. She explained how the houses in some places are raised above the ground because of the river or floods or rains. That night I couldn't resist testing out the teacher's information on my dad. We talked about the house in Cambodian, of course. My dad knows no American. The next morning in our class meeting, I took the book the teacher had read and turned to that stick house, built high up on its long legs. I explained how it wasn't built that way because of water at all. It was for the shade. I told them how on very hot days, the animals could stay cool under the house and sometimes even the family slept there. I explained how my dad had told me this. The teacher was very happy. She thought I was very clever to have checked out her information with my dad. She said she had learned what she said from a book, but my dad was the expert. I was proud of my dad!

On the last day of school, I felt sad that I wouldn't see my friends and the teacher for a long time. We talked about things we remembered from the year. We read old stories we had written. We got a paper back that we had done on the first day of school. I could hardly recognize my sketchy print and the sad, hollow self-portrait that I had done on that day so long ago. As the bell rang, the teacher held the door for us to leave, just like she did every other day. Many of the other children gave her a hug as they passed. John did. I passed her with my head low and said my usual, "Bye, teacher." I wish I could have hugged her, too. But she knows!

# DESK HANGERS

*Linda Fernsten*

High schools are a conglomeration of many unique individuals and groups. The adolescent group I call Desk Hangers is a breed apart, but perhaps more common than we realize. Unlike bouncy elementary-age students and exuberant junior high kids, some older teens have learned there is a price to be paid if they are seen bonding with authority figures, especially teachers.

I was in teaching quite a while before I even began to recognize Desk Hangers as their own entity, quite apart from the overzealous Chatty Cathys, who usurp your entire twenty-minute lunch period with endless details about anything, or the teens who continue their therapy session in your presence with different chapters of their bizarre adventures.

No, Desk Hangers are different. They're rather ghostly and easily missed if you're not on the alert.

I was huddled over the usual stack of papers the first time I caught one out of the corner of my eye. "Hey!" Michelle called in. "Hey," I responded, my eyes only momentarily diverted so as not to lose my concentration. Two minutes later she was back. Much as I liked her, I had three more hours of paperwork and was wishing I had closed my door. But . . . she didn't have Chatty Cathy tendencies . . . and rarely arrived late in the day like this . . . and had never before intruded when I appeared busy. I decided to give her full-face attention. She smiled as I made eye contact, inquired politely about my newest class, and gave a hurried synopsis of her day—but didn't leave. I set my pen down with just a shiver of reluctance. "Remember when you talked about your grandmother?" she plunged. I nodded. "Mine died this weekend." She forced an artificial smile and continued. "Everyone said it was best because she had been so ill. Nobody seemed very sad when we buried her but . . . " She hesitated, her voice cracking ever so slightly. "I don't know, I just thought I'd tell you because . . . " She didn't need "becauses" for me. The hug she didn't know she came for was waiting at my desk.

The quiet tears of shared experience were more important than grading tests that day.

Desk Hangers don't always know exactly what they want. They trust us to help them figure it out, sometimes wordlessly.

A Desk Hanger of another sort took me a while to recognize. Pete was usually the last one into class and the first one out—even on days when he sat farthest from the door. His code was clear: wherever the other side of trustworthy and understanding was, adults were there. I caught him paying attention a few times, though, when the subject of racism emerged in our discussion of *To Kill a Mockingbird*. A few students openly shared vivid experiences with it in ways that surprised him. His code of "Never Volunteer," however, prevented him from joining the discussion. "Has anyone ever been involved in or witnessed racism?" I prodded, glancing his way, giving him time. "People around here are always nice," he hurled sarcastically, but went no further.

That day Pete was not the first one out of class, and if Chatty Cathy had not filled the entire four-minute passing time with a detailed analysis of her latest trip to the mall, he would have been the last. During lunch I went to close my door and there he was again, pretending to fumble at a locker. On impulse I left the door open and went back to shuffle papers. Sure enough, when the halls were empty and no one could witness his behavior, he entered our class in that unsure swagger common to boys not used to passing time with teachers.

Desk Hangers often aren't sure of you or of themselves. Leaving out unneeded amenities, he looked around and blurted out, "A bunch of men drove by me downtown and yelled, 'Hey, Nigger, you dirty up our town.' I didn't want to say it in front of all the kids, but I wanted you to know." It's against Pete's code to be anything but tough, so I knew no warm fuzzy hugs were in order here. It was one of many days I wished for Merlin's wand to wave away the hurt and ignorance in our world. "I'm glad you told me," I said instead, and the only fifteen minutes of real conversation we ever had ensued.

Desk Hangers have a way of educating us and roping us to our jobs with invisible knots that let us know some fifteen-minute periods can be more important than 180 days.

One of my favorite Desk Hangers came back to visit me last week. "Favorite" is a term best used in retrospect, and Jose was no exception to that rule. The year I had him he was thorny and arrogant, streetwise and usually absent. I gave my annual speech about sophomores having an unusually high dropout rate and told them to look around, all of them may not be here to go on to eleventh grade. Jose was on probation, the terms of which prevented him from dropping out immediately, but he wouldn't anyway, he quietly assured me. His desk hanging had its own unique form. Under the guise of borrowing books by Latino authors from my personal lending library, he would lure me into private Desk Hanger conversation about his school attendance—or lack thereof. At least once a month, he'd goad me into hauling out my tough-guy lecture about "choices in this world" and other parent-like sermons. Still, back he'd come the next month, returning Piri Thomas and coaxing out another lecture.

Well, he finally did quit school, and, all my words to the contrary, it hurt to lose him. His apparition-like visits ceased, and he disappeared—along with a number of my books.

Last week, as I was teaching, I heard a knock on my door. No longer a boy, Jose strolled in and stuck out his hand to shake mine. "I came to say hello," he said with uncharacteristic confidence. "You won't believe this, but I'm in college now, criminal justice." He then addressed my startled sophomores, saying, "When this lady tells you to get off your lazy ass, get to work and listen. There's lots of junk out on the streets, but an education helps you through it." This year's crop was shocked into silence. A peer, not a teacher, speaking these words made them powerful, more real. As for me, no hello had ever so surprised me, nor had life's ironies ever felt so good.

This old Desk Hanger had reminded me in perfect fashion that the well-planned fifty-minute lesson we often obsess about is just one piece of the strange and complex job we're asked to do. There is no doubt about it, Desk Hangers have much to teach us—if we can only find the time to learn.

# STAYING AFTER

*Beverly C. Lucey*

The day was the third beauty in a row. You could lie down in the May sun and get tanned, and at the same time a breeze would keep you from sweating. You could get tanned. But *she* couldn't. Donna was in the detention room until 3:30 instead.

She settled herself with a great deal of noise, just as the bell rang to signal an hour's worth of enforced silence. This fuss was created to annoy the teacher on duty, yet was not flagrant enough to cause more official trouble. Donna knew her business. She had worn her clogs and couldn't help it if they clicked and thudded on the floor, now could she. And she just *had* to open her large cloth bag and take everything out, placing it all on the desk—a romance novel, used Kleenex, Bronzeberry Ice lipstick, her keys, some rolling papers—so she could find her purple Flair pen in case she wanted to write something.

She looked up at the teacher, Mrs. Foley, and found her staring, looking as though she was waiting for something to get Donna on. Donna stared back for some long seconds, gave in slightly, and began putting her belongings away. She jangled the keys into the bag, shaking the purse to be sure they hit bottom. She wondered if the teacher even knew what rolling papers were and covered her giggle with a cough as she dropped the packet in the aisle so those around her would notice and perhaps cause a disturbance. A few snorted quietly but this did not cause a response from Mrs. Foley, who was looking up, but not quite at anyone. Really. It was confusing.

Donna picked up the old, frayed Kleenex, opened a part of it and reused it, blowing more loudly than was needed, but hey! A person needs to blow her nose sometimes. What can anyone say?

She shifted her weight from one buttock to the other. Only ten minutes had gone by. This was the pits, a really gay way to spend the time. And anyway she shouldn't have had to serve a whole hour for trying to sneak out of Miller's class a couple of minutes early. If she hadn't got caught she could have met Chris out at the back entrance and had a quick drag. Really. English was so boring and she wasn't learning anything anyway and she hated being treated like a baby by some·dumb-ass teacher.

From her seat in the center of the room, Donna looked around, aching for something to happen. One boy, Dwayne, was sound asleep. His clotty snores were getting louder. Maybe the teacher would wake him up. Donna remembered once the art teacher had done it, woke Dwayne up in drawing class, and Dwayne had instinctively thrown a punch. Came from his brothers always going after him at night, she'd heard. Besides, everyone liked the art teacher. He was the only cool one in the school. Picturing Dwayne belting Mrs. Foley entertained her for a few minutes.

This other guy, Carl, was sitting behind a big guy, carving a piece of leather for a belt. He was making a mess on the desk and the floor, but he was quiet. Linda Mullion was blowing bubbles, but that dopey teacher wasn't saying anything so far. How do you ever figure what teachers will react to? Pete Garranga was writing "THIS PLACE SUCKS" in big letters on a piece of art paper. He was decorating it with bolts of lightning and snakes ready to strike. The colored markers occasionally screeched against the paper.

The big guy in front of the leather worker burped very loudly. Almost everyone jumped and laughed nervously. He was huge and new to the school. The kids called him Poker. Donna didn't know why. He was beefy but kind of cute.

The detention room teacher stood up all of a sudden and screamed, "That's eee-nough! out of all of you. I don't want to hear one more peep out of any of you or you'll stay here until four. Now, you've been warned. I trust I've made myself clear."

She sat down in the squeaky chair causing a pretty rude noise herself, Donna thought. If any of *them* did that, they would have gotten hell for sure. It wasn't fair. Then Donna looked over at Poker and saw that his face was red. He looked like he wanted to say something brutal to Mrs. Foley. His mouth was moving, but nothing much was coming out of it. Go on, go on, Donna willed him. Do it. Say something. She was excited at the possibility. But the color in his face went away, and Donna hunched over with disappointment. Ten of three. Bummer. She thought about standing up and in very specific, hard-edged words telling the teacher off, insulting the morals of the vice-principal and getting every single one of the kids in the room to follow her out, with dignity, heads high and maybe only one raised middle finger as a parting shot. That would be decent if only she could carry it off. The kids'd be talking about it for weeks. It might be worth five days of suspension . . . but did she dare? Uh-uh. No way. There was a field trip to the courthouse tomorrow and a party in Child Lab the day after. Bad timing to get tossed out now. Jason, the boy beside her, took off his flannel shirt in response to the stuffy atmosphere. He wore a black T-shirt with white lettering that said "Coed Naked Hockey. On the Ice Is Twice as Nice." Donna quickly looked at Mrs. Foley, who was reading the boy's chest through narrowed eyes. It looked to her as though Foley was mad and confused at the same time. Probably didn't get it. And if she did, she was trying to figure out if there was a rule against it. Yeah, well, what about the Constitution? What about *that,* Mrs. Foley? Mrs. Foley wrote something down on a piece of paper.

The room was quiet for about ten minutes as students slowly slumped over their desks, giving in to lethargy and the acceptance of the inevitable. Then someone went by the room and pounded on the closed door, jolting everybody into varying stages of alertness, even the sleeping Dwayne. There was laughter far down the hall as Foley seemed to debate a move toward the door. She apparently gave up that idea, but now the room was alive with restless movement. One boy yawned, stretched sideways and grabbed for the belt that Carl, the art student, was holding. Poker turned around to ask Carl for a pencil. Linda Mullion popped a big bubble. Jason, with the T-shirt, screeched his desk over a couple of inches so he could lean against the wall. This was forbidden. No one could sit against the wall facing sideways.

Mrs. Foley's head snapped up. Her eyes were glaring. She couldn't pinpoint all the noises. "Mr., uh, Stavon," she said to Poker. "Turn around."

"I was just getting a pencil."

"I said turn around." Poker snatched a pencil from the desk behind him and glared back. The art student was leaning to his left, trying to get his belt back. Mrs. Foley screamed, "Keep your hands to yourself, Carl Yonis."

"But it's mine, Mrs. Foley," Carl protested.

"Don't talk back to me, young man."

"Hey!" Poker interjected, "It's his belt. Look at all this crud on his desk. He was workin' on it all period. It's his belt. Leave 'im alone, why don't ya."

Mrs. Foley walked over and looked at the shavings and stain marks on the desk. "This is outrageous. You may be excused from this room. I'm telling the vice-principal about this vandalism, you can be sure." She turned and walked back toward her desk.

Poker grabbed the leather strap, wound it around his arm, got up carefully and followed Foley. Donna was incredibly excited and indignant. Poor Carl was in trouble for nothing. It wasn't fair. But much more interesting was Poker's menacing steps behind Mrs. Foley. Carl stood up, not really understanding if he was to leave. To leave or get kicked out of detention was an automatic suspension. In-school suspension was a nightmare: two days of total detention with only books and blank paper allowed, no paints, no projects, no nothing. He just stood in place, hoping she would change her mind.

Mrs. Foley reached the front desk, turned, and looked up to see Poker looming over her, snapping the leather belt. She made a little gasping sound in her throat. Jason, leaning against the wall, said, "Get her" clearly, but without moving his lips at all.

Poker stood there, flicking the leather, and said, very quietly, "That guy din't do nothin'. I got him in trouble for the mess but I din't mean to. Don't kick him out. OK?" He said this carefully, evenly, but Foley's eyes were fastened on the strap. The noise of it was the loudest thing in the room. She stood her ground, though, got to give that to her. "Don't you threaten me, young man. Maybe they did that in the school you came from, but not here. You won't get away with it here. You think you're so big, standing there like some delinquent. I know your type."

It was like a shot when the leather hit her face. She jerked backwards against the chalkboard. Yellow dust clung to the back of her pink suit jacket. Her knees were giving way. "Get out," she whispered, holding on to the part of her face that stung.

"Get out, all of you." Her voice cracked as she looked toward the phone that connected with the office.

Poker slowly moved to the door, flapping the leather loosely now against his hand. With a nod of his head he indicated everyone should follow him. The boys all got up. Some hurried after him. Carl used his hand to sweep up the leather shavings and put them in the basket. He looked back at Mrs. Foley but couldn't seem to figure out what to do next, so he walked out the door.

Linda Mullion and Donna were left sitting there. Mrs. Foley stared at them with watery eyes. Linda's eyes started to fill up in response but she shrugged it off, picked up her books and bag, then walked to the door and shut it quietly behind her.

Donna stared at Mrs. Foley, who by now was sobbing as she leaned against the blackboard, one hand clutching at the chalk tray. "Hey, Mrs. Foley?" Donna said. Mrs. Foley tried to focus her attention on this voice, this person. "If I leave I get suspended and I didn't do anything. You can't get me in trouble if I stay until 3:30, so I'm staying. You better sit down. You look a little weird. There's only ten minutes left anyways."

The corridor was quiet for about a minute after the last locker slam and the door opened slowly. Carl stood there, the belt hanging out of his gym bag like a gutted snake. "Mrs. Foley?" He moved hesitantly into the room and over to the desiccated woman. "You want to come with me? The nurse is still here. I checked. Someone ought to have a look at that." Mrs. Foley looked up blankly, as if she didn't recognize this particular boy, this gentleman, as if she had forgotten everything before the attack. "Why, thank you, Carl. You have always been a nice young man. I have often thought that. And . . . "

"Let's just get up now, huh, Mrs. Foley. Come on." He eased her up and held her lightly on the elbow for balance, the way he walked his grandmother to church. Donna just watched. She watched them slowly leave the room, then she watched the clock. When it hit 3:30, she left, slamming the door behind her, unredeemed, but free.

# WHAT'S IN A NAME?

*Richard Schaye and David Summergrad*

Diversity exists. It is a fact of our daily lives, one that surrounds us. In a bygone era we mythologized diversity out of existence. The dream of the arriving immigrant was to become homogenized and indistinct as part of the great American melting pot. It's not hard for any of us to find relatives in our past who changed their names to blend better into the American landscape. Today we are asked to acknowledge, recognize, and respect our diverse pasts and honor the richness that comes with that diversity. It is important that the educational leadership in a school helps us remember this. The weekly bulletin at Wayland Middle School recently included this letter from the principal:

Dear Parents,

One of my surprisingly enjoyable daily tasks is to read the names of the six students whose turn it is to have lunch duty. If your son or daughter has not told you, every day six students and a faculty member join the permanent clean-up crew (the custodian on duty, the study hall aide, the assistant principal, and myself) to clean the cafeteria. Each student whose name is read cleans up for two days; we go through all the names in a third of a school year, and then we start the list again.

Almost all the students do this task with good spirit. "Fun" might be an exaggeration, but we do manage to have a pretty good time while helping to keep the school clean. The few students who complain usually stop pretty quickly when they see the rest of us working.

I enjoy reading the names for two reasons. First, it gives me a chance to learn the names of all the students in our school. (I am lucky that it's for two days and it's repeated three times in the year—my memory needs continual reinforcement.) Second, I am fascinated by the names themselves. They collectively remind me of what is so special about being an educator in America. Each name tells a different story about our past; all the names collectively tell a story about our present and future. We have first names from Abigail to Zoe, with Emily, Jennifer, and Nicole mixed in with Asante, Rana, Seesun, Crystal, and Aurora. We have last names from Adams to Zeskind, with Brooks, Brinkerhoff, and Mikulski mixed in with Ganapathi, Hernandez, Qian, and Yanowitz.

I have a feeling that most students take all of these names for granted; it is what they have known from their earliest days of school. I am not sure they are in as much awe as I am that we have nineteen flags flying in our cafeteria representing the birthplaces of our students and staff, from Argentina to Zimbabwe, and that this week we ordered twelve more, from Australia to Sierra Leone.

In a world torn by civil war, it is special to me that our students accept each other as Americans, think of all these names as "no big deal," and aren't particularly surprised by our richness of cultures. For me, our names are special. In a holiday season celebrated in diverse ways, I am thankful that we have the freedom to celebrate as we choose, and I am proud of the educational responsibility we have to create from the many stories our common heritage and our common future.

I wish you all a peaceful winter break.

Richard Schaye
Principal

# WE TEACH THEM ALL

*David Summergrad*

The air is filled with laughter and the smell of new bought
books,
The schoolyard scene is hopeful, yet it's tinged with anxious
looks;
September is upon us, fresh scrubbed faces, glistening, clean,
Children gather noisily, greeting friends so long unseen.

Fresh starts imply another chance to learn and to impress
With a newfound positive attitude, crisp pants, a special dress;
The summer's magic lingers in the morning schoolyard air,
The brightness of a new year not yet tainted with despair.

They come from houses large and small, they come from near
and far,
Arriving on their bicycles, disgorged from bus and car;
Each child brings so much promise, so much achingness to
know;
An eagerness to question, a strong desire to grow.

Yet each arrives with baggage, often hidden from plain sight,
The pain an empty belly brings, another sleepless night;
Some come brimming with confidence, with privilege, with
poise,
Some come with fragile psyches, quiet girls and timid boys.

One youngster stands apart, divorced from all the rest
His fists jammed into pockets, face sullen and depressed;
One girl wears a worried look, her eyes are moist and red,
She wonders while she's here at school, "Who'll get mommy up
and fed?"

The bully looks about him, reassessing all his prey;
One child fidgets nervously, while others push and play;
Some youngsters carry weapons, hidden in their bags or clothes,
While others carry only fears beneath a valiant pose.

A gathering, several hundred strong, awaits the opening call,
To enter and begin the day, lined up there in the hall;
We ask the children first to strive, to struggle then to reach,
Christa McAuliffe told us: "I touch the future, I teach."

We see the children through a lens of optimistic cheer,
As teachers we encourage them to grow throughout the year,
The cycle does begin again, tradition every fall
The public school's ambitious pledge: to try to teach them all.

The schoolhouse opens up its doors to each and every one,
The morning bell has sounded, a new year has begun.

# REFLECTIONS

**diane danthony:** Writing "The Hardest Class Ever" has deeply affected my teaching on two levels. It is not just that the poem is about teaching and about students; it was also my first real writing experience. I started writing it two years after I had this class. The essence of the poem and the force of the words pulled and pulled at me, demanding my attention. I labored over each word, bringing it through numerous revisions to its present (and probably not finished) state. Doing that taught me more about the process of revision, which I require from my students, than any writing text or any workshop could. For me, becoming a writer was the critical ingredient in being able to help students become writers. And my frustration with process and product has helped my students see that writing is immediate, natural, and personal and that it has the force to capture any of us.

**Beverly C. Lucey:** I don't write to inform when I write pieces like these, I just feel stabbed by a moment or overwhelmed by the enormity and disparity of the lives in front of me, beside me, around my desk asking for Band-Aids, making excuses, bullying their way to the front of the circle, begging for cough drops and some kind of attention. Remember the opening of *Winesburg, Ohio?* Anderson says something about having dreams of faces floating in front of him and has come to believe they are the faces of people who need their stories told but can't do it themselves.

**E. J. Miller Laino:** I noticed the student [in "The Principal Makes an Exception to the No Hat Rule"] coming down the corridor right away because the "unlawful" hat called attention to her. As she came more clearly into my view, I noticed how pale she was and realized she'd probably had chemotherapy, since it looked like she had little or no hair under the hat. I also noticed that other students had stopped to stare at her. The hat was the first signal that something was wrong. One look at her fragile condition indicated, of course, she was wearing the hat for a reason. I was struck by the silent onlookers, students who didn't agree with the "no hat" rule and were trying to get the rule dropped. They had little respect for the rule, but they understood why this student was wearing her hat. I like to think they would have joined her in this hat wearing, not to break the rules and drive the principal crazy but to connect to a fellow student in her lonely ordeal. . . . It is very difficult to side with students in a situation like this, especially if those adults in charge are not open to other ideas. My motive in writing this poem was, I think, a way of speaking out, not just for the students but for myself and what I believe in. I guess I thought if I could accurately and honestly capture the situation, it might give some principal somewhere an insight she or he didn't have before.

**Diana Callahan:** The piece "Ratana's Story" originated in my own learning process in serving as Ratana's teacher. I underwent many personal changes and came to a greater understanding of what it means to support learners from diverse backgrounds as I reflected on my own behavior and interactions with Ratana. The teacher who was "shaking her finger" and using angry words at the beginning of Ratana's story was a far cry from the one who valued his explanation of the "stick house" at the end of the piece. I learned to see Ratana's behavior from his perspective and to understand it in the context of his own background and culture rather than to simply react as if it were inappropriate behavior.

Certainly, this piece and the events recounted in it have made me question how we view learners from diverse backgrounds (children and adults) in our schools and institutions. Often these individuals are seen as less—less intelligent, less experienced, less capable. Ratana was often viewed by the other children as "stupid." One could often hear comments like "Aw, he doesn't even know that!" It was very satisfying to see the entire school's change in attitude when Ratana was double promoted.

**Linda Fernsten:** I think writing about Desk Hangers and giving them a name made me more consciously aware of their existence. The teaching days take so much energy that we often have to run on automatic just to survive. Putting [students'] stories on paper keeps me thinking, makes me stay aware that there is no automatic pilot for many vital things in our job.

**Richard Schaye:** I wrote the piece on names for my every-other-week newsletter, which always starts off with a column from the principal. I chose the subject of names because I am fascinated with the wonderful sounds of names that I notice every day when I am calling out the names of students who have lunch duty on a rotating basis. I wrote the letter hoping my readers would be as surprised and delighted with the diversity of the names as I am.

# II

## Who We Are

We are students of all ages, from Jane Katch's kindergartner Nate with his "Two Teeth and a Tigey" to old don Pedro in Sylvia Shaw's "Across the Field." We share moments of truth that are at once unique and universal.

SYLVIA SHAW: *When I started to write "Across the Field" I wanted to focus on that magical moment teachers love, that moment when you have the class's full attention. They wait and listen, and for as long as that moment lasts, they are yours. You can teach them anything. I remembered one such moment clearly: my first day in the military academy. It was the day I fell in love with teaching.*

*As I attempted to recreate the experience for the essay, other memories found their way to the paper. Diverse experiences. Diverse students. Remembering my elderly Hispanic students, especially don Pedro, brought a different focus to the essay. Half way into it, I suddenly realized that in teaching him literacy, he had taught me what teaching is about.*

We are students and teachers who have come from far away.

RIC CALLEJA: *My poems are motivated by a need to understand my past, the crucial events that have shaped my present, like having to leave the town I was born in at the age of twelve, like having to learn English in a hurry as a teenager living in Boston. . . . Writing in short forms imposes a wonderful discipline on my writing. It challenges me to distill my stories and observations to the essential. Writing poems challenges me to think about words, their weight, their sounds. It's an economical way to write about one's life. . . . I keep on writing, "sounding my barbaric yawp," because I do not want to be voiceless.*

We are students who court or choose death. We are teachers who try to reach them and are forever touched by them.

DEBORAH SAVARINO: *A public school teacher with a parochial school background, when faced with a crisis such as suicide or issues of life and death in my classroom, I learned I could not impose my beliefs on my students. I had to listen wholeheartedly to their views, religious and nonreligious and, when asked, share my view without the rules and regulations of a particular faith.*

# I.M.O.B.

*E. J. Miller Laino*

He went out in a *hot box,*
just like he said he would
in his English composition:
*Your Life Ten Years from Now.*
Did his pen move across
the white lined paper
as brazenly as the stolen car
he drove wheeled around a rotary
smashing head-on into a ten-wheeler?
He only wrote a few paragraphs,
sensing, perhaps, he had already broken through
the way a football player
breaks through a drum-tight circle
of paper on Homecoming Day,
arms raised high, fists clenched,
crowd cheering, the space behind him
curling like the edges of a fallen leaf.
His hair was Huck Finn red.
The scar on his neck
came from a stray bullet he caught
during a gang scrimmage.
He only raised his hand once
during class discussion:
*If I ever got my girlfriend pregnant,*
*I'd never leave her or the baby.*
The cops said he had enough percocet
in his body to kill a horse.
A former student remembered
Brett's composition: *The way he said*
*he was going to be dead, we thought*
*it was a joke.* Brett's brother

described the party after the funeral.
Friends lit a bonfire, got drunk,
scattered joints in front of the grave.
Then they painted I.M.O.B. on buildings
all over town. In Memory Of Brett.

# CIRCLING THE DIFFERENCE

*Susanne Rubenstein*

He comes to me in a soft puff of air. There is a moment of tension then as he awkwardly, breath by breath, maneuvers his bulky wheelchair through the door. I am aware of twenty-four pairs of student eyes watching the scene intently from inside the classroom. I am aware too of the anxious eyes of those outside the door, his entourage of private nurse, social worker, and counselor. Mostly I am aware of the eerie hiss of his ventilator. The momentary panic I feel curiously transforms itself into a need to be unrelentingly cheerful as I greet my new student.

"Matt," I beam, "I'm so glad to have you in this class!"

By March I realize it is the truth.

But now it is January, the start of a new semester. My Creative Writing class is full of lively seniors already counting the days to graduation, a smattering of juniors eyeing them with envy, and one young man in a wheelchair, a quadriplegic for the last twelve years. Hit at the age of seven by a speeding car, he has spent the intervening years in various hospitals and rehabilitation centers. The decision to now attend public high school was his alone and provoked a fight he fought hard to win, and so even on this first day, while I am apprehensive about the situation, I recognize what a courageous young man he must be.

There is a flurry of activity in the front of the classroom. We scurry to find the best place for Matt to position his wheelchair, mindful of his impaired vision. A student in the front row gives up her desk, turning it over to the nurse who will remain with Matt at all times. We make space in the corner for the weighty bags that accompany Matt, filled with his books, computer equipment, and medical apparatus.

Practical matters temporarily resolved, the other adults leave, tossing me and Matt smiles of encouragement. The plan is simple. I have been told that my job is to conduct first-day-of-class business as usual.

No particular mention is to be made of Matt or his condition. Despite the fact that my students either are unable to take their eyes off of Matt or are politely refusing to look at him, I am responsible for convincing them that he is not different. That is the law. Matt is aware of his rights and is adamant that they be respected. The message is clear: In the classroom all students are the same.

For a while I take the message to heart. Boldly I urge Matt to plunge into the brisk activity of the class. He is assigned to a response group, despite the fact that his classmates have difficulty understanding his speech. He keeps up with the whirlwind of works-in-progress assignments characteristic of this workshop course, even though his short-term memory impairment sometimes makes it difficult. He participates in student-designed class presentations, even those that demand hands-on actions of which he is not capable. And he writes his autobiographical pieces, the core of the first class project, although the memories must be too painful to imagine.

It is a testimony to Matt's courage, his good nature, and his wonderful sense of humor that he does all this so successfully. So too is it a testimony to the humanity of his classmates, who welcome him and treat him—*almost*—like just another teenager. But he isn't just another teenager. He will never kick a soccer ball; he doesn't party every Friday night; he can't sneak off to the boys' room for a cigarette. While his classmates chafe at the restrictions living at home under parental rule brings, Matt lives closely monitored by machine in a hospital, wishing he could go home. Although both Matt and his classmates are engaged in a constant struggle for independence, their definitions of that word are worlds apart.

And yet within this classroom all students are the same. We do not acknowledge that Matt is different. That is the plan.

But we all know what happens to the best-laid plans. Reality intervenes. Matt is out of school for a time with an infection, and my students are concerned and question me about his condition. Occasionally within the classroom there are moments when his medical equipment malfunctions, and students sit frozen when the nurse jumps into action. Then slowly Matt starts talking to individual students. Always easy with me, perhaps the result of having spent so much of his life with adults, he begins to open up to his classmates, particularly to an irreverent and charming young man who delights in Matt's wit and no-holds-barred humor. I watch amused as the two begin a friendly competition for the title of Class Clown. Their jocular verbal jousts and edge-of-outrageous asides fill the classroom with laughter, and I feel the anxiety I've carried within myself this semester lightening, and then one day, in one quick burst of air and words, Matt himself blows all of the tension away.

His rival's comments have gone too far. Matt rears back in his wheelchair, shoots him a threatening look through twinkling eyes, and demands in a voice as strong as I have heard him speak, "Am I gonna have to . . . get up out of this chair . . . and . . . "

The class erupts in laughter. Score one for Matt. In my mind, score one hundred. With that one comment, Matt broke a barrier that all of us were guilty of building day by day. Suddenly now we all acknowledged the truth. Matt is in a wheelchair, and there are many things he can't do. The reality of that statement allowed us, however, to acknowledge an even greater truth. Matt is a human being, and there are many things he can do—among them wear the crown of Class Clown.

The title serves Matt—and the class—well, for a while. The students are more relaxed with him, and their banter has the ring of genuine adolescent camaraderie. But I wonder if his classmates are aware of where Matt's humor comes from, that it is at the heart of his survival, that it has carried him through years of terrible physical and personal struggle of which they are only vaguely aware. It is not my place to tell them, but I know it is something that they should learn.

The seniors graduate in May, leaving behind a tiny remnant class of eight juniors, including Matt. Although I imagine at first they feel somewhat like the proverbial party guests who have overstayed their welcome, it isn't long before the group develops a brand new personality of its own, and many of them, perhaps before a bit intimidated by the spirited seniors, begin to open up, speak out, and share their work in ways they wouldn't have before. Encouraged by the affinity they seem to feel for one another, I decide to let them talk about writing through oral presentations. We form a tight circle, Matt's wheelchair marking its beginning and its end, and we listen to one another.

One Tuesday early in June it is Matt's turn to speak. The assignment: to talk about a piece of writing that has had a powerful impact on you. Matt has told me in advance that he has chosen a piece of inspirational writing given to him by his mother not long after his accident. The background to the piece is vague, but the effect it has had on Matt is not. I suspect his reading of the piece and his comments on it will move the class. Little do I know how far it will take them.

The sun is streaming in the windows that June day, and the students are gazing expectantly at Matt. They have grown more accustomed to the breathy timbre of his voice through the ventilator, but still they watch him closely, following his lips. Slowly, with the airy pauses that indicate his nervousness, he introduces the piece. Then he stops and I watch him take in all their faces. Perhaps he sees the compassion in Ellen's eyes. Maybe he notices Steve is sitting up straighter. And maybe he knows the look on Kevin's face is like the high-five given to a teammate. Whatever the reason, Matt makes a decision, and when he begins to speak, his voice is sure.

"I think . . . " the ventilator puffs, "it's time . . . " another burst of air, "to tell you about . . . me." We stare, mesmerized.

And so Matt tells us his story, the facts and the feelings of twelve long, arduous, painful years. No one moves; we barely breathe. I see tears in Marcy's eyes, but they are not tears of pity; they are tears human beings shed when they share a moment of complete empathy. And when the last word comes from Matt's mouth, Kevin rises and says, in a voice thick with admiration and respect, "Good job, man."

As the last few days of class wind down, it is clear that finally Matt has been completely accepted by his classmates. I hear it in the ease with which they now ask him questions about his past—and his future.

I see it in the flirtatious smile one of the girls gives him as she pops a last-day-of-class homemade treat in his mouth. I know it when one of the boys talks about a near-tragic athletic injury and says quite simply, "Matt would understand how scared I was."

Diversity in a classroom is a wonderful thing. As we learn to understand and accept differences in others, so too do we learn about ourselves. Matt taught me and those seven students that important lesson. And he taught me something else too—that in order to accept differences among human beings, we must first acknowledge them. Although perhaps it seems easier to tell our students, "We're all the same," it is a lie. Matt *is* different, physically and emotionally, and to ignore those differences is to ignore the real Matt. That would be the tragedy. The young man my students and I came to know—because he had the courage to say "Let me tell you who I am"—is an extraordinary person. He is neither just another teenager nor the young man in the wheelchair. He is Matt, a person as unique as each of the seven students who shared a circle with him.

# DANCING DOWN THE STREET

*Nancy Allen*

Having to hide who I am used to be a way of life. What if they knew? Would I be fired? Teaching high school, I was worried and then scared when I saw the word written in big letters with an arrow pointing towards my desk: DYKE—a word to strike terror in the heart of any lesbian teacher. Fifteen years ago, when I taught high school, I was just coming out to myself and had never heard of the word homophobia, internalized or externalized; but both were very present during the three years I spent in that institution.

The first year at the high school, my third year teaching, a number of incidents happened that made me want to leave the profession altogether. When a male student, whom I didn't know, followed me down the street one day whispering, "Dyke, dyke, dyke" repeatedly under his breath, I kept walking. I didn't turn around, didn't think of reporting him, didn't think, just felt, felt like crying, did cry, felt like crawling into a hole, hiding—where? Finally, after what seemed like a mile but was really only a few blocks, the whispering stopped. I turned around and he was gone. Did I imagine it? Am I crazy, I wondered. No, I knew what I had heard.

Another day that spring I walked into my most challenging class and found a note on my desk from a senior who was one of my most difficult students. Now, I would put it away and read it later or ask the writer to speak with me privately, but then I did neither of those things. I read it. She wrote that she had heard I like women. She and others had been discussing this rumor and wanted to know if it was true. She assured me that they would like me either way, they just needed to know. All eyes were watching me as I read. I kept my face still and told her I would speak to her after class. I don't remember what I taught that day. I do remember how exposed I felt, how afraid and vulnerable.

When she met me after class, I denied who I was for the first time. I said that I had many women friends but they were just friends. I did not say, "What makes you think my personal life is any of your business?" as

I might now; or, "Yes, I'm a lesbian. Does that clarify things for you?" as I would like to now. I hid who I was, and I felt much shame and loss in doing so. I found my ally, the one close friend I had there, in her library office. I fell apart and she listened quietly, responding in the only way she knew how: "They're just kids. You couldn't have done anything else."

Why not? I wondered.

At the end of May that year, Northampton's annual Gay and Lesbian Pride March was held. I wanted to be part of it, but I was fearful of the consequences. What if a student or parent saw me? What if my picture was in the newspaper and everyone saw me? Most gay teachers whom I knew went out of town for the weekend to avoid this internal conflict. Some stayed for the march and wore masks or bags over their heads. One high school teacher, head and body completely concealed, felt the need to borrow shoes from a friend so her own would not be recognized. I wore a mime costume, complete with white face. No one knew who I was, not even my friends. During the march I kept having to introduce myself to people I knew well.

I didn't stay long. I was drained emotionally and physically. I left the happy, cheering crowds to go to my quiet, safe apartment. I didn't realize how much I had been holding in until I got in the car. Then I fell apart, crying and dry heaving. Hiding had made me sick. I vowed then that I would never march again until I could do it openly without shame or fear.

During the past fifteen years, I have been facing that fear in myself and others. Taking a "Heterosexism and Homophobia" course sponsored by Equity Institute helped me confront my own homophobia, and it gave me a support network so that I could begin to confront it in others. This support gave me the courage to attend a Gay, Lesbian, and Straight Teachers' Network (GLSTN) conference in Boston and to come out to my superintendent and my principal, who was and still is very supportive.

Over the years I have come out to my faculty individually and collectively, and have encountered both positive and negative reactions. With the support of allies and friends, I have been able to let go of much of my fear. Now I am part of a committee to keep schools safe for gay and lesbian students. I include families with gay and lesbian parents in my family unit for second graders. But I still do not feel completely safe.

Last year when a sixth-grade teacher and I were doing a unit on prejudice, which for the first time included homophobia, I felt that I had to hide again. For many of these students it was the first time they had used the word "gay" as a descriptor rather than a put-down. There was plenty of homophobia among the students, but I kept questioning their attitudes and assumptions, hoping that they would see the connection between racism, which they understood is wrong, and homophobia, which they had been taught by society is acceptable.

We had finished reading *Number the Stars* by Lois Lowry and were discussing the Aryan race and who Hitler chose to be deported into concentration camps. We had talked about the yellow star and the pink triangle. One Jewish girl said, "I would have been chosen." A disabled boy said, "Me, too." A boy who had in the past asked me many questions, such as "How do you know if you're gay?" and "How do you become gay?" looked directly at me and asked, "Ms. Allen, would you have been chosen?" I replied, "I have blond hair and blue eyes." This time the hiding was a deliberate choice, but the pain of denial was the same. The discussion went on; the moment had passed. Would it have been safe? I never found out.

Is it necessary for me to come out to my students? I think it is important for me, my students, and society as a whole. To be the best teacher I can be, I need to be free of fear and open about who I am in order to establish trust so students will feel it is OK to be who they are in all their uniqueness. It is important for students to know gay and lesbian people personally in order to counteract the stereotypes society has presented to them. Finally, it is important for the community to acknowledge, encourage, and value diversity if we are ever to become a country that reflects its proclaimed ideals.

Last year during the annual Pride March, I danced down the street in my cowgirl boots behind a truck blaring country-western music. I was a member of the Despurados, a dance performance group, and we drew much attention. I danced with pride. The tears this time were ones of joy.

But I still need support from heterosexual teachers and administra-tors to be able to answer students' direct or indirect questions with hon-esty. My colleagues can be allies by confronting homophobia in all its forms, not only in their classrooms, but also in the faculty lounge and in the community at large. With their support, the next time a student says, "I don't know anyone who is gay," I can answer, "Yes, you do. You know me."

# THE BONES

*Joel Levine*

The healthy understanding, we should say, is not the argumentative, but the intuitive, for the end of understanding is not to prove and find reasons, but to know and believe.
—*Thomas Carlisle*

My student walked into the resource room looking more than a little apprehensive. Accustomed to the crestfallen visage of the chronically school-frustrated adolescents who were my stock and trade, I settled back in my chair. "Problem?"

"Yeah, I guess so," Danny said, making no eye contact and shuffling his feet.

"Do you want to talk?" I leaned forward.

"I want to show you something." He paused. "No, it's probably not right for school," he decided, and started to head for his desk.

"Look, Danny, if you have something to show me, I'd really like to see it, but it's your choice."

This was typical of Danny, as shy and guarded a young man as I'd ever taught. He had a long career of getting by with his strikingly handsome features, neat appearance, and ever so quiet demeanor. I often felt these assets worked against him, for despite his massive deficits in language comprehension and reading, people responded mainly to his appearance and overlooked his glaring difficulties in learning. Danny was complicit in this. He often downplayed both his needs and his frustration with learning by avoiding commitments at school. He was unable to express ideas in a way that corresponded to his feelings. As a teacher, I often felt my expectations of Danny reflected back to me as a kind of rudeness, and I was overwhelmed by a conflicting impulse to "just leave the kid alone."

I started back to my folders.

He hovered around the desk. "Maybe I should show you in private."

"Is this something that could embarrass people?"

"Oh no," he said. "Well, not like that."

I decided to bite. I cleared the folders away, leaving a space on my desk large enough for what I expected to be some futile written exercise or exam.

Instead Danny hauled up a wrinkled shopping bag and plopped it on the space. He reached into the bag and took out what appeared to be bones. As my eyes widened, he quickly looked around and produced four, five, then six bones.

My initial surprise dissolved into uneasiness with each successive retrieval from the bag. Something creepy was happening, possibly illegal and unhealthy. These weren't chicken bones; they were much too large.

As a teacher of students with special needs I have learned that inquiry, when called for, is pursued along a very delicate line. Accuracy of recall and sequence can easily congeal into a mishmash of vagueness and evasion where threat to self-esteem is perceived. I intuited the fleeting and rare element of pride in Danny's disclosure.

"Danny, do you know what these are?"

He replied matter-of-factly, "They are the bones."

He said *the* bones, not just bones. "Where did you get them?"

"I dug them up."

"Where?"

"In my back woods."

"Do your parents know?"

He paused. "I don't think so. Only you know."

I felt drawn into a conspiracy by a student who probably didn't know what a conspiracy was. "Tell me, Danny, how did you know they were there?"

"Because I put them there."

"You did—"

"Yes, I buried Max a couple of years ago." He gave me that look students sometimes have that says at once, "Don't you get it, and if you don't get it I'm outta here." He started to pack up his bones.

"No, wait, Danny. Who is Max?"

"Max was my dog."

"But why?" I felt regret as soon as the word escaped my mouth. It came out as an accusation. I could have guessed that Danny might not be able to construct a reason and was in fact looking to me, the teacher, to give him one, though I had no idea what his actions could mean.

"I don't know, maybe I shouldn't have brought them in," he said.

I was losing him. Reflexively, I touched his arm. "You do know, but you are not feeling you can tell me." At that point I needed his assurance more than he needed mine.

Now he looked surprised. "I just wanted to see what would be left in the ground after two years."

My rationality gave way to intuition. My goodness, this was show and tell—the pure excitement and enthusiasm of little children when they bring some part of their life into school. They share it, then it's done with.

For Danny no more embellishment to his explanation was necessary. I joined my own curiosity, now freed of suspicion, to his own sense of wonder: "Well then, are there more?"

He brightened. "Yeah, I didn't bring them all. I have two bags."

"Well, I suppose you are aware of the hazards of decomposed animals? You may need gloves; there must be a proper way to handle these." I was on a roll. "Yes, it's exciting, perhaps you'd consider doing some homework around this."

The situation was on the verge of cliché: "Yes, class, it's Washington's birthday, who wants to write a report?" In this case, though, there were no collective moans; homework validated Danny's experience. It was OK to dig up Max because a teacher would be interested.

It was not hard to empower Danny after that. Making metaphors of Indiana Jones looking for lost buried treasure, teaching the word archeology, shellacking and wiring together bones in the resource room normalized the experience for all who came in contact with Danny over the next three months.

He did, in fact, go to see a professor of paleontology and wrote a field trip report in his clumsy, labored script. Somewhat later, Danny got a job and a truck. He put school behind him and moved on in the world.

Max no doubt sits somewhere in town, meticulously reconstructed and whole, as my student who by accident of neurology could not be. I return to my well-worn classroom habits and bide my time in anticipation of the next dig.

# NEW LANGUAGE

*Ricardo Calleja*

All through that winter, my first,
I had no language for the external world.
My own, the one I still prayed in,
was useless in dealing with strangers.
At the playground, I blocked when they said to pass
and passed the ball when they yelled "Run."

At my desk in Saint Gabriel's,
the hours passed slowly
as words flew past me like flocks of noise.
But devoid of words,
I learned to read faces,
to decipher eyes,
to smell the essence of intentions.

# TWO TEETH AND A TIGEY

*Jane Katch*

"Eeeeee!" As Nate's cry pierces the classroom all motion stops, as if we were cars on a highway stopping at the sound of an ambulance siren.

"What's the matter, Nate?" I say.

Why do I ask? The children in my kindergarten class don't ask. When they hear Nate's cry, they immediately look around them. If Nate's orange and black striped tiger, "Yellow Jacket," is anywhere in the room, it is sent flying over the toys, straight to him. I know what's the matter when I hear him cry. I ask because I wish he could tell me.

I am getting better at understanding Nate's speech. He leaves out many sounds and makes substitutions for others, but he is a patient teacher, repeating what I don't understand, substituting other words, even giving me definitions. But the idea that he could stop and talk with me in his moment of greatest distress is a wish far from today's reality.

On this day, Tigey does not come flying across the block area. Nate bursts into tears and runs into the hall. I hear a momentary pause as he checks his cubby. The wail starts up again, in the direction of the playground.

I look into the hall. Nate is gone, but a teacher is passing by.

"Do you have a minute? Nate's upset. I think he's gone to the play-ground to look for Tigey." It's a small school, and everyone knows Nate and Tigey.

They come back soon, Tigey held tightly in Nate's arms.

I watch Abby brush her teeth at night, and I notice two white bumps sticking up behind her lower front baby teeth. Instantly, I know I've seen them before, but refused to acknowledge their existence. How can a four-and-a-half-year-old be getting two permanent teeth?

"It hurts here, too, Mommy." I look at the back of her mouth. Two molars are coming in.

She's excited the next morning, anxious to tell her friends, but cries when we say good-bye, the way she used to do last year.

When I pick her up at school I say, "Are you still my little one, even with two big teeth?"

"Yes." She smiles. "But I have four big teeth."

Abby has always looked older than her age. She's tall enough to pass for at least six. She was through with diapers at two. She talks and plays like an older child. Will she get her period at eight or nine, before either of us is ready to face puberty?

In a small math group I'm working with the concepts of longer and shorter, following the kindergarten unit in our math series. I bring out a set of small plastic links, used for measuring, comparing, and counting in almost every unit. I ask each child to make a chain with them so we can compare lengths. Two children grab piles of links, connect them, and argue about whose is longer. Quickly, Nate starts to cry, and says he can't do it. I watch him struggle to hook the two links together. My teacher's manual doesn't tell me what to do if a child can't put the links together.

I can do math without links, but can I stop comparing Nate to the other children, wishing he looked more like a kindergarten child?

Since Abby could stand up, I've been looking for a child her age as tall as she is. Some years, she's only in the ninety-fifth percentile, so why can't I find the other five percent? Other years, she's off the chart. "Will she be a six- or seven-foot basketball player?" I ask the doctor.

"Maybe not," she answers. I am not reassured. People who meet her and are told her age say, "She's so big!" I always answer "She's tall, but she's still my little one." We both like that.

"Put your name on this list if you want to tell a story. I'll write it down and later we'll act it out," I explain to the class.

Nate comes over to me later. "I'm not old enough," he says. "You write my name."

Later in the day, I read *The Biggest House in the World* by Leo Lionni. The children are fascinated by the story of a small snail who magically makes his shell as large as a cathedral, only to find he can no longer move around or find food.

When I'm done, several children take large pieces of paper and paint huge, colorful snail shells. Some use clay to model snails, while others choose their usual activities of blocks, sand, and pretend play. After a while, I walk over to Nate, who is working at the clay table. He's made a tiny but perfectly coiled snail.

How can he do that so easily when he can't connect math links and is afraid to pick up a pencil and paper?

"Play the egg game," Abby says when she wakes up in the morning. She curls up into a large ball in front of me.

"I wonder what this baby will be like when she's born," I say. "Will she like the baby doll I'm saving for her? I do hope she likes to snuggle. Will she want Ninja Turtles to play with? I don't have any Turtles."

Eventually she's born, and I find she likes baby dolls, snuggles, kittens, and macaroni and cheese. We go into the kitchen to make my coffee and her hot chocolate. "Pretend I'm the mom and you ask me if you can drink coffee," she says, holding her mug just the way I do.

"Can I please have coffee, Mom?" I ask.

"No, dear, you're not old enough," she responds gleefully.

A tragedy at our school. A ten-year-old girl has been hit by a van and killed. We are all upset, but Nate and his mother were especially close to the family. Nate has been angry and unreachable all day. While I read one of my favorite books on death for young children, Nate loudly shoots imaginary guns in the block area.

Finally, before dismissal, he says, "I'm so sad Tara is dead." His straightforward comment opens the discussion for many who have found it hard to talk.

As he goes out the door he mutters, "It's so 'tupid that people die. It's so 'tupid."

"It is stupid," I agree. I try to hug him, but he slips away.

Is Nate changing, or do I see him differently when I'm not measuring him?

Snuggling close to me in bed in the morning, Abby says, "It will be a sad day, the last time we snuggle like this."

"You can snuggle as long as you want to," I say, missing the point.

"But some day will be the last day," she goes on, undaunted by my lack of understanding.

"Why will that be?" I ask.

"Because I *am* going to get married and have babies, you know. So the day before will be the last day."

She'll be ready for adolescence whenever it comes. I'll have to work to catch up.

"I need 'Ellow." Nate comes up to me at playtime and leans against my arm.

"Yellow paper?"

"No. 'Ellow 'Acket."

"I'm sorry, I don't understand. Can you say it a different way?"

"My Tigey. 'Ellow 'Acket."

"Oh, Yellow Jacket! Has anyone seen Nate's tiger, Yellow Jacket?" I announce to the class, interrupting the play.

One very worn, much loved stuffed animal comes sailing toward us.

Nate tucks it under his arm and smiles at me.

# ENDURANCE

*Daniel Murphy*

*For my student, Chhouk Chhouy*

When darkness set in,
you raced
for leaves and berries.
While they were away
in magic land,
in camps,
in graves,

black night helped
you to eat.
Your swollen belly
was filled
with roots.
You were just seven,
all grown up.

# PIECES OF OUR SOUL

*Deborah Savarino*

Annie Zorya died this week. Was there part of my teacher training in undergraduate or even graduate school that addressed this issue? Did I miss that lecture? Similar to the unspoken wish that parents should not bury their children, there is an equal wish, a hoped-for, silent agreement between teachers and students. As parents, there exists a part of our soul in each of our children. As teachers, it happens that way with some of our students. Do we bury that piece of our soul when they pass from this earth? As Annie's mother's tears burned through my shoulders, I did not have words. I could only hold her.

The distressing vision of Annie rose before me as I walked the halls of the high school. I was filled with apprehension. I carried this distraction for days from the moment I was notified she was in a coma as a result of a drug overdose. From that blurred moment, I knew it was a matter of time. We had lost track of how many attempts she had made on her life. "You'll see, someday I will be gone."

Images of the past came into focus. One day after class, she stood quietly by my desk. "Ms. Sav, why do all my teachers say these are the best years of my life?" This stopped me in my tracks. I had to think about it carefully before answering. She waited with a pained expression. Slowly, I said, "I think their memories are colored by time. When you look back over the years, there are so many best times that they outweigh the bad times."

Now I try to remember the best times with her, days when she was pleased with her schoolwork and her creative writing. If you could be a child's toy, what would you become? "Playdoh," her journal said. "It brings my little brother such happiness." Then there were days when she would rather frolic in the park across the street from school than be in the classroom.

Suddenly, regular school was too much for her. After another suicide attempt, she was placed in an institution with a psychotherapeutic component to help her. I noticed an improvement. I can still see her laughing with her peers in the adolescent unit. "Look at these thunderthighs. Look, I can pinch the skin on my fat waist." Her peers began to affectionately call her Chubs. She was beyond the point of being convinced that 94 pounds was not even close to fat. Perhaps her thinness was an attempt to vaporize into thin air.

Annie worried about evil, its charm, its pull. I once gave her a Kachina doll she admired and told her it could protect her from evil . . . then I went home and prayed. But the horror in her life pulled her in too deep. I remembered all the rides home from our tutoring sessions when it would take all my psychic energy to clear her clinging, negative, depressive air from my heart. I prayed harder. I tried to trust the medical establishment. We collaborated on the best literature selections for therapeutic value. I also tried to reassure my students, the peers she had left behind. They were scared, confused, wandering lost in their own attempts to make sense of Annie's suicidal ways and their own journeys through adolescence. One of my students admitted in horror, "That could have been me!"

It could have been me, it could have been us. Many of us have been balanced, poised on that threshold of the dark doorway where two worlds collide. What is it that turns us around to choose life? Our class discusses this. As we share tissues and tears, I only have my own personal answers to offer them. There are wings that protect me. They are woven of individual feathers of love from friends. Their iridescence and lightness are a reflection of God's love. This love is what shields me.

Annie, I'm sorry you couldn't fight this anymore, sorry all the psychotropic medications and therapies couldn't get you past the pain of this world. I'm sorry you only saw the sorrow. I regret I could not convince you of a world that holds incredible joy as well as devastating sorrow. How does a teacher impart such critical knowledge among the curriculum guides and lesson plans?

As I stood, arms around my other students, at her funeral—a place you never envision while you are preparing to be a teacher—I cried.

Unashamed of our feelings, we all cried. Tears of a curious mixture: pain, separation, horror, frustration, anger, and deep sorrow. Through this sea of tears, I see you, Annie, somewhere better than this place . . . perhaps frolicking in a celestial park. Perhaps it is as one of your peers said, "Maybe next time she will get a stronger soul."

# ACROSS THE FIELD

*Sylvia B. Shaw*

I didn't know what I wanted to do with my life, only what I didn't want to do with it.

I stayed up most of the night trying to decide on a career. After all, college sophomores are supposed to have some notion, at least the night before they have to declare their major. With paper and pencil, I tried a stream-of-consciousness tack to try to get at the inner me that was aching to be born. Who am I? What am I going to be the rest of my working life?

The task of creating that person, then and there, was daunting. I wonder why I thought she had to be completed before dawn.

I scribbled the night away in a spiral notebook, rattling on about how much I liked architecture and writing and traveling and French and pre-Hispanic art and classical music and Spanish lit and being alive. Then I read my ramblings. Through the steam of a second or third cup of coffee I saw that I liked more things than I could possibly major in within the limitations of a Bachelor of Arts degree and my modest finances. Certainty #1: I liked too many things equally to be able to focus on any one thing. Certainty #2: I was determined not to be a teacher.

My father was a teacher, one of the most dedicated, inspired, over-worked, underpaid instructors in academia. I wasn't going to fall into the same trap. Not this eager, ambitious, frightened sophomore!

I set my clock and slept a couple of hours. Then I sat in class and filled out the form. With steady, unwavering hand, I declared my major: Teaching. Secondary Ed. Foreign Languages.

I did not question the contradictory, fatalistic tenor of my decision. In the absence of certainty I had opted for intuition. I now felt like a hiker freeing herself of a heavy backpack at the end of the trail. Decision had given me focus; college became a gourmet meal on an empty stomach: Spanish and French entrees, ed. courses and student teaching.

In my senior year I was given sole charge of two courses at Valley Forge Military Academy. The school had an enrollment of eleven hundred students, grades seven through junior college. I was the only female instructor. On my first day on the job, cadets in tight-fitting wool uniforms craned their necks to look at the oddity in high heels. They jammed the doorway and buzzed excitedly. The seventh graders stood at attention when I walked into the room. I wondered wildly if I should salute back or simply beg them to sit down and relax. I had enough presence of mind, and years in the military, to say coolly, "At ease!"

Chairs scraped noisily against the floor as they sat down. Then I found myself gazing into the faces of little boys far from home, kids with faces polished like their boots, children as timid and eager as their teacher. They waited in a silence loud with expectation. As I stepped into their field of attention, so perfect, so riveting in that first encounter, I knew why I had chosen this career, this moment.

In the twenty-one years since that day, I have stared across many such fields, gazing into the faces of Hispanic women eager and frightened to learn English, freshmen at Clark University anxious to survive their first college English course, and high school students interested or bored with Spanish. So many faces, most friendly, some hostile, so many days of elation and frustration. But never the thought that I should have done anything else—well, only momentarily, when a student's rudeness knocks the breath out of me. My jaw shakes as I send the offender out of the room. The bell rings. The next class comes in. Young faces look up into mine, after I've hushed them up. And sometimes a sense of expectancy, almost as perfect as that first one, takes hold of me again, but with an added dimension that came only gradually.

I remember my dad complaining in his gentle, tired voice about some of his students; other times he glowed. One evening he told us about a football player in his music appreciation class.

"I was playing Tchaikovsky's Sixth Symphony," my father held his fork in midair. "The kid sat there transfixed, tears rolling down his cheeks. After class he came up to me and asked, 'Where can I find more music like that!'"

My dad's eyes moistened as he smiled and returned to his food.

That's the added dimension I didn't know about when I first fell in love with teaching. It's not just the "I have something wonderful to teach you," but the reciprocal gift from student to teacher.

It's what old don Pedro gave me years later when I taught him how to read and write his native Spanish. One day he handed me a spiral notebook. With the penmanship of a fourth or fifth grader, he had carefully filled some twenty pages in pencil.

"I've written the history of my village!" he beamed at me.

No, I should have told him then and there. You've done so much more than that.

# MY TOWN, SAN LUIS, CUBA

*Ricardo Calleja*

I used to ride from one end to the other of my town, San
Luis.
I could go from El Entronque to Las Cuatro Esquinas
Down Calle Cespedes all the way to the park
On a girl's bike.
But in the third world no one ridicules you
for riding a girl's bike.
They admire you for having wheels.

From our porch across the tracks
I would nightly see the parade
of trains carrying their sweet cargo
to one of eleven sugar mills
that spewed black dust,
but breathed life on San Luis.

In San Luis I could play checkers
with Gil the barber and watch Modesto and Raul
work their magic on a 57 Chevy
and keep it running
despite revolutionary slogans,
despite the American embargo,
with home made parts.

And on Sunday nights I would walk
clockwise in the park with Rolandito
and check out the girls walking counter clockwise
dressed in the Sunday's best
In my town, San Luis.

# REFLECTIONS

In a compelling postscript to her story, "Circling the Difference," **Susanne Rubenstein** demonstrates the learner within the teacher: "Yesterday Matt donned a cap and gown. With a bright yellow balloon tethered to his wheelchair, he spun himself in circles, a broad grin on his face. When 'Pomp and Circumstance' began to play, Matt joined the procession, heading toward the future. I watched him proudly, thinking of how far he'd already come—and thinking too of the distance he had carried me.

"In a suburban high school, even in the nineties, diversity in the classroom tends to seem more a concept than a reality. In twenty years of teaching, I have had only a handful of students who appeared not to have been cut from the same white, middle-class mold. As a result, both my students and I have been somewhat complacent, imagining that we all shared a similar background and experience.

"When Matt appeared in my classroom that first morning, I was not thinking diversity—or maybe I was. What I was thinking was, 'How do I deal with a student who is so different from his classmates? How do I make him comfortable with them? How do I make certain that they treat him well? How do I guarantee that they learn from one another?' Maybe those are the questions we as teachers encounter when we try to create classrooms that respect diversity.

"It was Matt who taught me the answers to those questions, and the answers were a surprise to me. My experience in dealing with differences in the classroom was narrow; consequently I thought the simple, good-hearted response of 'We're all the same inside' was enough. Now I know it's not.

"Now I know every student in a classroom is different. Some of those differences we see—in the color of the skin, in the contours of facial features, in the tremors of the body in a wheelchair. Some of those differences we hear—in the syllables of a foreign tongue, in the singularity of an opinion, in the puff of a ventilator. Some of the differences we feel—in the hesitation of a response, in the sadness of the student who sits apart, in the frustration of a young man whose memory just won't work for him. And some of those differences we never know because our students have learned too well how to hide the things that make them unique.

"Knowing Matt and reflecting on my experience with him has taught me this: difference must be acknowledged. It is only when we recognize the differences among our students—and ourselves as teachers—that we can appreciate the diversity that is the human race. Matt is not like any other student—but neither is there truly a category called 'any other student.' Every student is unique, even those students who seem to be cut from that same white, middle-class mold. Though all our differences may not be immediately visible, they are there inside in the experiences that have shaped us and made us who we are. As a teacher I believe it is my responsibility to treat each student as an individual, cultivating those qualities that make each one unique. As an educator I believe my job is to nurture individual differences, to guide my students in an appreciation of these differences, and only then to begin to help them find some common ground. From now on when it seems easier to gloss over the differences, I will remember Matt confronting his classmates with the story of his life and I will remember the boy who said, 'Matt would understand how scared I was,' and I will know that moment of empathy could not have happened had Matt allowed us to pretend that he was not different.

"For me and one fortunate group of students, Matt pushed that door wide open. My thanks to him is a promise that in my classroom it will not close. From now on we will delight in the differences among us. We will form circles of diversity and perhaps we will spin as joyously as Matt on graduation day."

# III

# What We Learn

Along with science, language arts, social studies, physical education, and other subjects, some of what we learn is about ourselves and each other. Some of what we learn is about taking risks.

We are students who learn English while we learn all the other lessons of school. In Daniel Murphy's "A Cambodian Girl's Lesson," the significance of the past tense takes on new meaning. We are teachers who recognize that if we expect our students to engage themselves to learn what they should, we might just need to strive and cross some boundaries of our own, too, like the teachers in Tess Boyle's "Butterflies All" and Amy Mann's "Marisol."

We are students locked into fear of taking risks. We are teachers who must help students unlearn what others have taught them, as in Catherine Desjardins' "Just James," where the teacher-speaker acknowledges for James his rightful indignation for the fourth-grade teacher "who threw things at people when they got the answer wrong." And we are teachers who remember our own teachers who did not support our first feeble efforts along the path of learning. We are well acquainted with the teacher in Jane Katch's "Red Tie Shoes" as she contemplates Tod's insecurity and reluctance to share his schoolwork and confesses that she relates to Tod's fears as she sits down to practice the piano during the evening at home. She sees in front of her the ghost of the piano teacher from her own childhood and how Miss Newton sighed and quickly took over the keyboard, humiliating her for her inadequacy.

Sometimes we learn more than we've asked for or ever want to know. In Beverly Lucey's "Shelley Gives Her Report," Shelley dutifully completes the assigned report on one of her everyday activities, breaking it into all the steps involved, describing each step in detail. And what about the Shelleys who aren't prepared to give their reports? (It's not because "the dog ate it.") What are they learning?

Both "A Cambodian Girl's Lesson" and John Hodgen's "For My Nigerian Student Who Will Not Believe That Men Have Landed on the Moon" attest to what there is to learn when we look thoughtfully into our students' eyes.

# A CAMBODIAN GIRL'S LESSON

*Daniel Murphy*

My Cambodian student's father
lost his hands, legs, head;
who knows what else.

I do know cargo
that floats,
and hurts

my blue eyes
when I have to look
into her dark eyes

that cannot look back.
My eyes flood
the green valleys

that she'll never see.
I bite my lip, then lecture
about the past tense.

# BUTTERFLIES ALL

*Tess Boyle*

Juicy Earthworm was the name they gave me in a workshop I attended years ago in which we gave each other Indian names. There was Soaring Eagle, Flying Pony, and Waving Sunflower, but I didn't care. I am an earthworm, sticking close to the ground, helping not hurting, round, slow moving, same old, same old. People like me are the ones depicted at the beginning of a movie. Then someone or something comes along, changes everything, and they find themselves flying with nothing but an umbrella or dancing down Main Street in the middle of a snowstorm in a gold lamé jumpsuit. I'm the before-the-epiphany person. It's not for everyone, but I like it. I like being solid, reliable, most often the backdrop to other people's epiphanies. It is so much fun to watch. Maybe that is how I ended up being a sixth-grade teacher, round, slow moving, daily witness to so many epiphanies. I feel one coming on now.

Perhaps you have heard of the Butterfly. I hadn't. It is a dance. When you do it, your legs move in imitation of the wings of a butterfly which fold up when it lands on something. There is a motion there, hard to describe, a light coming together of velvety wings, rhythmically folding and unfolding, opening, closing, smoothly touching, parting. So beautiful is this motion one just wants to do it. A motion, I might add, about which earthworms know nothing.

Now it would really be carrying the metaphor too far to say I have no legs. Of course I have legs, sturdy legs, with sensible shoes at one end and substantial hips at the other. They are usually covered by a blue pleated or gray flannel skirt with matching opaques in the winter. How did it come to be then that these beautiful little girls from Jamaica assumed that I could do the Butterfly?

It was that time at the end of a school day when we sit with our coats and bookbags and wait for someone important to say, "Bus students may be dismissed." It was at that waiting time when my beautiful little girls from Jamaica said, "Here's how you do the Butterfly. Move your foot like this and your knees like this." They look at me, sure that, with their instruction, I will be able to do it. The kid from Vietnam and the one from Poland and several other kids watch and listen, and pretty soon I am the only one not doing the Butterfly.

I try, so help me God, I try but my archless feet make it hard for me to move my heels without moving my toes. Unless that happens, the knees will not do what the wings of the butterfly do. Of course who will know under my navy blue pleated skirt? Is that me hiking up my skirt so they can inspect my knees? Tomorrow, I'll wear slacks. "Be sure and practice over the weekend," Takeysha says as the bus pulls up. I help her pull the hood of her jacket over the many brightly colored barrettes. "See you Monday," Nikki waves as she climbs onto the bus.

Will I practice over the weekend? Of course not. That is just something you say to keep the children feeling secure and to impart to them a sense that their teacher is interested in them and their Butterflies. Actually, except for those few minutes before church on Sunday and a couple more just before bed, I didn't practice at all. Strange as it may seem, it is possible to do that little heel-toe thing while standing at the sink washing dishes or even in line at the Stop & Shop. By Monday I was no better.

"She don't know how to weave," Takeysha whispers up to Nikki. She has this way of looking up at Nikki, her older cousin. "Don't make her feel stupid," her eyes say. Nikki's eyes grow round as if she has just been told of a creature who has grown to adulthood without knowing how to breathe. In my heart I know I'm doing something wrong. Funny, I thought I had the moving the heel thing almost right. Nikki gets the message about being kind and assumes a professional air. I know what's coming. I've done it so many times myself. "You did a great job on this paper but. . . ." "First you need to weave," she says to me. They both begin weaving, thinking, as they do, exactly what are the steps in this process. OK. When they think they have it, they show me, explaining each step slowly, evaluating the level and speed with which I am able to process the information. Weaving, I discover, is a way of moving the hips. "Back, left, front, right. Back, left, front, right." These are my ample hips I'm moving. The faster I do it the more ridiculous I feel.

I'm coming to the end of my comfort zone when they both yell, "Yes! Yes! That's right." My comfort zone extends itself. I begin to notice that as I move my hips a wave courses up my spine causing my shoulders to go back and forth. Well, actually, it is more of a circular motion. "You weavin', Ms. Boyle. Look, the teacher's weavin'!" The rest of the kids come to watch. They begin to weave too. "Now weave your arms too." I do. We all stand there and weave together for a while as my confidence grows.

Takeysha and Nikki look at each other as if to say, "Is she ready for the next step?" but just then the bus announcement comes. We weave our way out to the bus. "You the dancing teacher?" the bus driver asks. "No, but she will be by tomorrow," my instructors shout. "Practice!" they all shout to me as they climb on the bus. Takeysha runs back to whisper in my ear, "Monday, you got to weave and Butterfly too."

# JUST JAMES

*Catherine Desjardins*

The first day of class, you disbelieved our
silliness, playing an alphabet name game.
When it came your turn to match
an adjective with your name's first letter
you growled, "I'm James. Just James."
Two people past you, I realized
you'd done what you'd been asked
and so you became Just James.

Is it harder for me to meet your eyes,
skittish animals ready to dart away,
or for you to meet mine as I flitter, unsure
what to do to make you feel safe
somewhere you think you're an imposter?

Just James, the first time I made you write
the truth, instead of the clouds
of generalities and platitudes
you got by with for years,
you wrote about a teacher in fourth grade
who threw things at people when they got
the answer wrong, about a time he called
on you and the whole class watched you flounder,
until an eraser nicked you, stained you white.
After that, you stuttered for years.

Still, teaching you, I have to know, James—
Did you read the book? Did you do your homework?
Are you here with us?
We're on your side, James, like the girls who
clapped silently the first time you spoke in class
more than halfway through the term.
But we can't give it to you, do it for you, James
and I don't know how long to stand calling
under the darkening sky:
"Come in, James, come in. Ally ally in free."

# RED TIE SHOES

*Jane Katch*

Tod stares at his blank page, an expression of worry on his face. He holds his pencil so tightly his fingers are white where he grips it.

"May I see the picture on the other page?" I ask him. He lets me look at the tiny shoe in the lower left corner of his paper.

"Would you like me to write some words on it?"

It's the first week of first grade, and we're starting writers' workshop. I've shown the class a book that tells a story with only pictures, and explained to the children that the only words they must have on their first book are their own name and the title. I will help them with the title, if they want.

But Tod does not answer me.

I ask him to tell me about the shoe.

I can barely hear his answer. "Someone jumping."

I look at the next page. Two tiny shoes. "What's this one?"

"Someone running," the whispered reply.

"Should I write the word 'running'?"

"No."

He turns away, so I won't see him crying. I give him time to look out the window and get himself together.

"What you did is fine with me," I say. "You don't have to put any words on it today."

I walk away so he can look out the window some more.

I glimpse at my reflection in the window as I walk into the Vanilla Bean Café that night. I look good, I think, wearing my favorite Laura Ashley jumpsuit, carrying my story in my hand-woven notebook from Thailand. I've been imagining reading this story, my favorite, for weeks. It will be my first time in front of a "real" audience. A famous poet will be there to read his work, and before he arrives members of my writers' group have volunteered to read short pieces. Maybe he will come early and hear me, and he'll love my story and send it to his publisher.

I'm amazed and thrilled to see the Vanilla Bean is already filled. I look for a seat. I see an author I know a little. His second novel is getting great reviews. He's with a student of his, also a writer. There's an empty seat near their table. I hadn't expected to see anyone I knew, and suddenly my stomach starts to tighten. I ignore a friendly wave from someone in my writers' group, and head toward the empty seat.

"That's a beautiful notebook. Are you going to read?" the student asks.

"Maybe, if there's time."

The first reading is an honest but unpolished love poem. Author and Student at my table exchange knowing smiles and when the audience applauds they clap only two solitary, small claps, the bare minimum.

Student whispers to Author, with his hand in front of his mouth. I think he says, "Do you think it's any good?"

Does Author answer, behind his hand, "Not really"?

I take out a piece of paper and write a note to Sarah, who's organizing the readings, "Got cold feet. I can't read tonight. Maybe next year."

I dream that night. I am standing by a low table in a crowded room, reaching for a glass from a tray. I look great, in a slinky black dress. I know how to make sparkling conversation with strangers.

But why are they staring at my feet? I look down and see I am wearing Alexis's red leather tie shoes.

They know I'm an impostor, not a grown-up, after all.

At our morning meeting, Alexis answers a question and one of the boys in the back says, "Aw, everybody knows that!" I see Alexis's face change from excitement to shame. I say, "Let me tell you about something that happened to me." I tell them about my plans to read my story, my fear that the Author and the Student would smirk when I read and clap only twice, and how I took my name off the list of readers.

The children say, "You should of read anyway! Who cares what those guys think!"

I tell them I felt that way too, as I was driving home afterward. I was mad at myself for not reading, for letting their rude comments stop me. "I don't want Alexis or any of you to feel you can't say something here because you might be put down for it," I say. "Alexis, did you feel bad when someone said 'Everybody knows that!'?"

She nods.

"Let's be careful not to make anyone feel that way," I say, and we get ready for our second writers' workshop.

I walk around the room, watching the children gathering pencils, paper, stapled books. Tod takes paper and pencil and begins to print. It's tiny printing, starting at the top of the page and quickly filling up space. I try to glance casually at it as I walk by. I can read his phonetic spelling! "N somer mi famle went to man"—In summer my family went to Maine! After a half hour he gets up to put it in his writing box. As he walks past me, avoiding my eyes, I say, "I'd love to see what you've done, but if you want it to be private, that's OK, too." He continues walking past me, without a pause, to put it away.

I remember Tod's fear as I sit down to practice the piano at home that night. I've just begun to take piano lessons, and as I start to practice, I see in front of me the ghost of Miss Newton, the piano teacher of my childhood. I am twelve years old again, and when I play my first wrong note, Miss Newton sighs deeply. She sits down to play the piece correctly, her long red fingernails clicking on the keys with each note. My humiliation is accompanied by a brief resolve to practice more next week, which I know I won't keep. I'm wasting the money, inherited from my grandmother, that my parents are spending on my new piano and the lessons I had asked for but which I dread.

But now, things will be different. I am grown up. It's my own money. I don't have to practice if I don't want to. And my teacher, Julie, is a friend who appreciates my love of music and who does not wear fingernail polish.

At my first lesson, I see how different she is from Miss Newton. She appears uninterested in my mistakes, unless they indicate a concept I do not understand. In that case, she explains it to me and we continue. She laughs at a loud discord I play when I reach the end of my piece.

"You'd be surprised how may people do that," she says.

But I think a lot about my mistakes. While I practice, I imagine playing perfectly at my next lesson, my teacher telling me I am her most talented student. I plan my first concert. While making these plans, I am not concentrating well on the notes I am practicing, and I begin to make more mistakes. Each time I play a wrong note, I feel the whole piece is bad and start over, hoping for the perfection that eludes me.

Why am I so caught up in my mistakes? Why can't I, too, see them as something to learn from?

I am in third grade, sitting in the middle seat of the middle row, hiding behind a serious look, keeping my eyes on the teacher and my hands folded, as I have been taught. The teacher does not know I am pretending to ride a wild horse I have just caught on Assateague Island.

"Recite the seven times table," orders the teacher. In unison, we recite, "Seven times one is seven, seven times two is fourteen . . . " We move at a terrifying pace toward the hard ones, the eights and nines. I move my mouth mutely, pretending to speak.

"I think some of you don't know these. Come up here." She points to me and Anna, the stupidest girl in the class.

"Continue."

I cannot speak.

Near the end of my next piano lesson, I say, "Julie, I've saved the hardest part for last. I can play this piece pretty well, without too many mistakes. But I can't get much feeling into it, even though I love the music."

"Play it for me," she answers.

I play it well, with more feeling than I have been doing at home. It sounds terrific to me as I approach the crescendo. Then, BANG! A wrong note at the worst possible moment.

I know at that instant why I've been practicing the piece without feeling. If I play tentatively, it isn't as awful to make a mistake. If I put myself into playing the piece with feeling, I might suddenly realize I have on the red tie shoes again.

My teacher seems to read my mind. "Pretend you know how to play," she advises me. "Don't worry about getting the notes right. Then you can go back and work on the notes later."

At writers' workshop, Tod hunches over his paper, filling his page with tiny print. I sit down at the small, round table, talking to everyone but him, looking at their work, helping them.

"Would you like to read that to me?" I ask him, finally.

He nods, and begins to read. I am thrilled, but I can't hear him. He speaks too softly, and I see only the back of his head as he bends over close to his work.

Should I tell him I can't hear him? He may stop reading and never try again.

Maybe if we both pretend he's reading loud enough for me to hear, some day he'll read so I *can* hear him.

And maybe next year, I will read at the Vanilla Bean Café.

# MARISOL

*Amy Mann*

Marisol came to my class when she was fifteen. Her hair was long and dark, her skin a smooth, creamy brown. It was rumored that she spoke no English and that one of my colleagues had called her unteachable. I remember thinking that was an awful thing to say about any child.

That year I had a small ninth grade. Most of the students were challenged in some way. Ann and Kathy were traditionally special education resource room students being mainstreamed for the first time. Bob had many behavior problems. Laura was constantly declaring that she was stupid. The course I had designed for this ninth-grade English class was called "I'm Nobody, Who Are You?" and was to be an exploration in identity. It fit this group perfectly.

About a month into the school year, Marisol appeared in the doorway. Our eyes searched each other. What I remember most clearly about that moment was that Marisol and I had the same eyes: deep and dark and sad. If the eyes truly are the window to the soul, then I believe she and I had the same soul.

She stood on that threshold afraid to step in. I told Marisol my name and where to sit. There were brief introductions. I remember thinking, Why me? Why did I always get the kids others found "unteachable?" This class pained me. Each student so needy, so deserving. How would I manage? And now Marisol. No English. Lost in a country with so many white faces. How would she learn?

My teaching had changed in the years before Marisol came to me. I had enjoyed the "stand and deliver" monologue that brought attention and laughter from my audience. I had made the shift as more and more students seemed content to sit and listen instead of to think and stretch. Slowly I had moved, crossed the imaginary line between them and me, moved closer, asked what they thought and felt, what they hoped for and believed in.

In the year with Marisol, however, I learned more about the limits and boundaries of the classroom than I had in any year before. I knew she would not learn if I conducted business as usual, attending to Kathy and Ann, worrying that Bob would go off at any moment. And so I agonized.

I think most of us can remember those rare moments when we have been willing to let down our defenses, admit we can't do everything, and ask for help. I remember one of those moments. Marisol was sitting quietly, politely, waiting for me to be her teacher. The others also waited for me to be their teacher.

"I need your help," I finally said. "Marisol needs to learn to speak and write and read in English. What should we do? How should we teach her?"

Their startled eyes were piercing. In the silence of the moment I became uncomfortable. Then I saw their surprise and their delight. I have since learned to welcome the pregnant silences where some of the best thinking is done.

"Well, I read to my little brother," Ann said.

"Let's bring in stories," Laura suggested.

"We'll read to her," Kathy offered.

"We'll write stories together."

They amazed me. Despite their individual struggles to learn, they knew so well how to teach one another.

"Maestra, maestra," Marisol interjected. While we were busy planning her year, she waited to be told what all of this meant. "Ayuda, nosotros ayudamous." Help. We help. I think she knew what I was trying to say, and we began.

The room became a flurry of activity: a small group reading stories to Marisol in one corner, students reading and writing and preparing interviews in another. I began to notice that the usual boundaries between teacher and student, white and brown, English and Spanish seemed to have no place here. And though I didn't know it would happen, I watched as Ann read novel after novel. Kathy learned to write and to read aloud, Bob calmed down, and Laura showed us all how much she knew. And I stopped being afraid that I wasn't teaching.

The metamorphoses were spectacular. By Christmas, Marisol was reading at close to grade level, and although she continued to tightly clutch her Spanish-English dictionary to her body, I could see that her self-confidence was growing. The hair was out of her face. Her eyes were bright. She was making friends. How she had grown under the gentle care of her classmates!

The year progressed as any year does. There were bumps and bruises and name-calling of the racial kind. The small haven we had created in Room 16 could not protect Marisol from the subtle racism of our small, rural community. But the class was not held bound by it. We learned some Spanish. We learned about Mexico. And we suspended some of our old ways of thinking.

As the year drew to a close, we knew that Marisol would be leaving, returning to Mexico. That June I nominated her for the ninth-grade English award. I watched with pride as she walked up the stairs to collect her prize. Perhaps she accepted this on behalf of the class that taught her. She held her head high.

"Gracias," she said.

The day Marisol left, she handed me her dictionary, an offering of the boundaries we had crossed together.

I think about Marisol now as I struggle with other boundaries that I am not sure how to cross. I have lost touch with her, but her memory, her presence is strong. I am the keeper of the dictionary now. It is my gentle reminder of what is true about kids and learning and what is possible in school.

# SHELLEY GIVES HER REPORT

*Beverly C. Lucey*

It's Shelley's turn to face the class in the speech unit, and she gets up to give her report about a visit to her mother in a neighboring county last weekend. The assignment was on how to do an everyday activity, one we would all recognize but might never have noticed how many steps were involved in it, this ordinary thing.

Shelley moves to the front of the classroom, happy to sit on the teacher's throne—a contraption made of two stacked wooden chairs. She stands in front of these chairs and, with an expert backward jump, lands smack in the right place. She looks around at her waiting classmates, who wonder what that new girl might be going to talk about. Most of them have explained how to change a tire, how to clean and insert contact lenses, and how to program a VCR to catch a week of *All My Children.*

Shelley's hair is wild, and one eye seems to float sometimes behind her glasses, but she usually can reel it back just in time to answer a question or pack her books as the bell rings.

Today, as she skates her small hands along the legs of her jeans, she says she will report on how to deal with her mother when Lindy is around or if Dot turns up. Everyone in the class knows that Shelley is in a foster home, but no one knows much else about her, so she's got their attention. The mystery of families beats instructions about how to make whoopee pies.

"First of all," she announces firmly, "what you've got to do if you meet my mother is make sure you've got her alone. It's pretty easy to tell because she's got a great singing voice and when she's alone she sings all the time. When you've got my mother alone, you can get her to do most of what you want—like she'll take you down to the mall and get you stuff at the Gap and she'll make you lasagna because she is so happy to see you. She sings songs from Woodstock mostly, like 'Here Comes the Sun' and 'I Get By with a Little Help from My Friends,' which is the song you have to watch out for, because that's when Dot might turn up. Dot's a real bitch. She hates me and I just go up to my room if she's around because she belts me when my mom leaves. She calls me a pig and says my haircut is shitty and I'm draining the lifeblood out of the whole fuckin' household just by being there. Sorry, Miss Kimmini. Do I lose points for bad language if I'm quoting someone?" The teacher makes a small not-to-worry flap with the back of her hand from the back row seat where she sits.

"So," Shelley continues, "what you have to do to avoid Dot is go up to your room and not unlock the door. One time I thought it was Lindy, who's only six, knocking out there and crying, so I opened the door but it was Dot being a faker, and she quick got out this bungee cord and hooked my mouth by the cheek like some damn bass, you know? Dragging me downstairs and out into the yard saying I had to wash all the sheets hanging out there because a bird crapped on one of them. I just yanked them off the clothesline in a big, messy bunch and did what she said because I didn't want to cross Dot, but I sure was hoping my mother would be back before the social worker came or she wouldn't let me come out even once a month, I figured. Then Lindy came down in the cellar where I was running the washer and drier, saying she wanted to paint clothespin dolls with me, but I had to ignore her. It was getting close to four when Mrs. McCarthy from DSS was coming to check on all of us, so I just told Lindy to *please* go find mom or we'd all be in big trouble.

"Lindy promised she'd try, and by four the house was picked up some, Ma had made some pudding, and Dot and Lindy were nowhere in sight. See, you have to be real clear. That's the one thing you have to remember. My mom can do anything for about a couple of hours and all I can do is hope that the new medication can keep her my mother for longer and longer times. OK. That's about it. You want me back in my own seat or do any of you got questions?"

# FOR MY NIGERIAN STUDENT WHO WILL NOT BELIEVE THAT MEN HAVE LANDED ON THE MOON

*John Hodgen*

No, she says, and her eyes grow large,
two black moons, eclipsed.
I show her chunky astronauts, frolicking,
gamboling, one small step after another,
the blare of light like aureoles
on the round black visors of their helmets.
No, she says, they are men, nothing more,
and men cannot dance on the face of the moon.
The moon is so far and the men are so small.
Only dreams can go there
and the words that fly out of my heart.
The moon is the eye of the old one, she says,
still awake in the house of the night.
It is the mother who cradles us deep in our sleep.
And no one could walk on that face, on that light.
I look in her eyes and I know she is right.

# REFLECTIONS

**Daniel Murphy:** I combined, imaginatively, my students' experiences with those I had learned about when researching my Irish ancestry. One morning I awoke, walked to my desk, and wrote each poem. The page was spotted with tears when I finished them.

**Catherine Desjardins** (offering a postscript to "Just James"): James did do his homework. His writing improved dramatically, and his final growth statement in this course melted my heart. It showed how, though demeaned and mocked as a child, he constructed his own sense of self-worth, first through pride in athletics, then through his decision to become a teacher, a goal he constructed for himself with no real support or precedent. . . . James has taught me not to prejudge students. Behind his reluctant exterior is an extraordinary young man.

**Amy Mann:** The piece "Marisol" really began as something else. I was trying to talk about boundaries, mainly the boundaries in schools. I was messing around with a much more technical or maybe analytical piece in preparation for one of the Field Center's writing retreats. I brought the piece to my group, and my group leader pushed me to really tell a story about school boundaries. The Marisol story just poured out of me. I was completely surprised that this experience had such an impact on me. Telling the story of Marisol publicly reminds me that my teaching must stay student-centered. This is critical but easily forgotten. It raises questions: How can schools better meet the needs of *all* students? What kinds of professional development opportunities are necessary to help teachers be successful at creating healthy classrooms? How are potential teachers recruited and prepared to teach changing student populations? How can we change our limited or stereotyped views of students who are different from us?

# IV

## What We Bring

The stories and poems in this section suggest that our students bring many things to school. They bring all they are and all they have ever been. They bring where they come from and where they are heading. They bring with them all those who have made them who they are. They bring their parents, who stand by them, sometimes over them, with their expectations. They bring those who walked away long ago, whom they do not know. They bring the children, for whom they will try to stop being children themselves. They bring the "big kids," who beat them up. They bring their questions. They bring their answers.

# I ONCE HAD A STUDENT NAMED MICHAEL

*Nancy O'Malley*

I once had a student named Michael
He is the only person
I've ever known
Who was completely alone in the world
Given up at birth
To a woman he called mother even after she gave him away, too.
When most little boys were trying out two wheelers
Michael was trying out foster homes
And hospital stays on holidays.
There were long stretches of time
When the foster homes were replaced by shelters
And Michael learned to pack his things neatly
In a green plastic garbage bag
For quick transport
When there was no more room for him . . .


I met him standing outside my classroom door
A sad-eyed man boy with a crazy crooked smile
And lashes that
Gave him the look
Of some overdrawn cartoon character.
But they were real.
"I don't know who I got these from. I mean my mom or dad."
And that old man weariness
Would leave for a moment
And a grin would take over.
There was no answer for him
Just the reassurance that his eyes,
Like his agile mind,
Were a gift from God

But a gift that no one had claimed
Or was ever likely to . . .

One parents' night at school
Michael walked in dressed in a three piece suit
With the grin playing wide
"How'm I doing?" he inquired boldly
Looking over my markbook
"There's no one to ask about me, so I'll ask about myself."
Some of the other teachers were angry. Why allow this intrusion?
It was up to the staff at his group home to come.
"But they didn't."
There was consistency in that
They didn't come that night just the same way
No one came to claim him
On holidays when the group homes
Ran with a skeletal crew
And microwaved turkey dinners for the leftovers with no place
to go . . .

The last Christmas I saw Michael
He came with us to *The Nutcracker*
Almost missed the first act
Because no one at the home could sign him out.
But he came at last,
Rushing through the crowded street and snowbanks
Out of breath
The treasured suit all cleaned,
A red carnation in his lapel and clutching proudly
A rose for my daughter.
"You didn't think I'd miss my best Christmas ever, did you?"
I would like to know
Where in the universe
It gets evened out

Where do the Michaels
Get all the birthdays that were forgotten
Or missed or ignored or blown out without so much as a
Single candle . . .

I haven't seen Michael
Since that day when he disappeared
Down the crowded corridor and didn't look back.
Sometimes in the afternoon
When the corridor is empty and the light plays
On the far reaches
I look up and think I see Michael
Walking through the door
With his crooked grin and great deep eyes
And once, late last fall on a deep November night
As long lines of proud parents' chatter
And the urgency of loved ones filled the room
I looked up for a brief moment
And thought I saw Michael
At the end of the line
Proud and anxious too
Standing there for himself.

# LOSING YOUR PLACE

*Beverly C. Lucey*

Sunny wheeled the baby carriage past the guidance office, the band room, and the computer lab, heading for the detention room. She was looking for Chad, the baby's father, who had mouthed off to his marketing teacher the day before and now was supposed to serve an hour after school for the next three days. Her right breast was leaking, darkening a spot on her pink tee shirt into a raspberry-colored bull's-eye. For a moment she felt as though she might need to lie on the carpet in the Media Center and take a nap, but the feeling passed and she went on.

Inside the carriage, the baby, red in the face and capped by his mother's red hair, seemed to stare vacantly at her flushed face bobbing in front of him. Lockers slammed in an uneven series of crashes, and someone was pounding on a bass drum that had been left in the auditorium to her left. Sunny's head was coming off and she wanted to scream something like "shut up" at the whole school.

Two weeks a mother, and the foggy glow of the label seemed to be dissolving. Chad had promised he'd look for a job today so they could live together and she could get out of her parents' house. Sunny had read where smoke was bad for a baby, so even though she hadn't quit she figured that one smoker in a house wasn't as bad as four. Plus Eddie, her stepfather, now drunk about four days a week, and Irma, her grandmother, were at each other again—hollering and throwing things. Last night when Sunny was nursing Tyler, Irma shook a dry mop over Eddie, filling the den with dust. Sunny's asthma kicked up, and she kept coughing the baby off her nipple. Eight months ago, that first night after the wick turned pink, Irma'd lifted her always-filled glass and toasted her little grandbaby becoming a mama and a woman, in that order. Grammy Irma was the one who swore she'd kill Sunny if Sunny killed her unborn baby and promised to set her and Chad up somewhere if Sunny would only go on and do God's will. But Grammy kept stalling with the money she'd promised. Now, she just kept saying six months, six months before she could get her hands on that bond to change it for cash or something like that. Sunny was stuck at home for the duration.

Outside 101, the detention room, Sunny stood, rocking the carriage and trying to peer under the poster of a ski jumper that covered the window to catch Chad's eye. Four boys were asleep on their gym bags, one girl was reading a V. C. Andrews. The only other student in there was a girl named Jenn, who had helped her on a cake decorating project in freshman home ec before Sunny stopped coming to school in February. Finishing that carousel cake and giving birth were the only two times Sunny ever felt proud of herself in all of her fifteen years. Mostly she'd felt restless or tired since she was twelve. The detention teacher walked over and opened the door, glaring at her. Before backing off from this silent warning, she quickly looked in to be sure; Chad wasn't there. Two girls and a teacher each stopped to say hi and look at the baby while Sunny tried to decide what to do next. She thought the teacher had looked at her funny—like she was a slut or something. One of the two girls, Reenie, asked her if it hurt much and was it fun having a kid all your own.

As Sunny walked to the back entrance she saw through the long narrow side window a bunch of guys crowded around Stan Gorey's truck, then she thought she saw Chad's hat—a fedora among the team caps, sticking up behind the flatbed. Slowly she tried to maneuver the carriage through the heavy blue double doors. She had to turn around and use her butt to press the door bar down and pull the carriage over the metal hump.

Chad hadn't stayed over in about a week. He wasn't at his mother's, either. She'd only talked with him once, yesterday morning, when he said that for sure today he'd be going to the Star Market where a friend had put in a good word for him. He'd sounded impatient, though, like she was being a bitch for asking. Right now she mostly wanted a kiss.

By the time she turned around to head for the truck, the guys had spread out funny around it, like in a long line, and across the practice field she was sure she saw a small, stocky guy with a fedora running, running fast, without looking back. She pulled the carriage backward and sank onto a wooden bench. He hadn't wheeled the baby, not even once. Her eyelids drooped to a close as she tilted her head toward the warm, bright sky, her ears deaf to the baby hiccuping, oblivious to the other breast letting go, her mind as blank as it was the night it all started.

# SILENCE IS NO LONGER GOLDEN

*Eugenia M. Nicholas*

This past spring, I chaperoned a two-day school trip to the White Mountains in New Hampshire. On our second evening, the Appalachian Mountain Club guides took small groups of students on moonlight walks in the woods around Pinkham Notch, an experience that was the highlight of the trip for many. I stayed at the base camp with those who had sprained ankles, upset stomachs, or sore feet. I heard noise from one of the dorm rooms, and when I went to investigate, I found two girls who had returned early. One of them was huddled on the bunk bed, crying. When she was able to tell her story, she said the walk had triggered a flashback to a time in her childhood when she had been sexually abused by a family friend.

She was not the only one who told a story through tears. Shortly after we arrived, I stood beside the telephone while a sobbing girl begged her father to come and pick her up. This was her first time away from home, and she was terrified. The next two days were a series of barely averted crises, as she fought her fears and I supervised her medication.

Before dinner the first night, I saw another girl running toward the dorm in tears. She told me she had gossiped about a friend and hated herself because the girl didn't like her any more. She felt as if she had ruined her life and no one would want her as a friend again.

The boys, too, had demons to fight. At dinner I noticed a boy at a table across the room. Everyone around him was laughing and talking, but he had withdrawn. His head was resting on the table, cradled in his arms. He had come on the trip reluctantly because his father, whose business kept him in Africa for months at a time, was home for a brief visit. His parents had not wanted him to miss what they considered a once in a lifetime chance, but the boy had his own priorities. After talking with him, we decided that he needed to go home. His dad drove up to get him later that night.

Another boy came to me with a tearstained face and said that one of the bigger boys kept hitting him and was urging others to do the same. He said this always happened to him, so he knew there must be something really wrong with him.

I left the White Mountains feeling perplexed, wondering if I needed to be retrained as a psychologist, wondering if I had said the right things to any of these children. The teasing and insensitivity early adolescents could turn on their peers was not new to me, but my students were sharing their problems more frequently than they had in the past, and these problems seemed increasingly complicated. I mentioned my concerns to a friend who is not a teacher, and he was astonished that students would discuss their problems so willingly and so openly. "We used to keep things to ourselves," he said, "and we managed to get along OK."

In one respect what he said was true. Years ago, silence was highly valued. Children were supposed to be seen and not heard, and adults had a similar code of behavior. They did not "wash their dirty laundry" in public; what went on behind closed doors remained behind closed doors. Those were the days when curiosity about a neighbor forced one to resort to snooping tactics à la Jimmy Stewart in *Rear Window,* a movie about a man confined to his apartment with a broken leg who uses binoculars to spy on his neighbors. This code of silence was encouraged in private, too, by parents who subscribed to a "stiff upper lip" philosophy and had neither time nor patience to listen to children's woes.

In the last few years this code of silence has been eroded as we have scrutinized not only the lives of public figures, but also those of private citizens, be they soldiers fighting for our country, victims of natural disasters, or family members grieving over a tragic death. Adults have bared their souls in newspapers, magazines, and on talk shows. Children have listened and watched, and now they are mimicking these adult models.

On the last day of school, the girl who had been homesick ran up, gave me a big hug, and said, "Thanks for helping me." I was startled by her words, for I certainly hadn't solved her problem and in retrospect it didn't seem as though I had done much except be there. And then it occurred to me that perhaps that was what she had needed more than anything else.

Relief flooded through me, and I felt a renewed sense of purpose. When students reveal their feelings, they are taking a positive action to help themselves by acknowledging—and forcing us to acknowledge with them—that suffering silently does not make suffering disappear. The girl's words of thanks reminded me that most children do not need a psychologist. They need someone to support them as they break the code of silent suffering; they need someone who will anchor them when they are riding an emotional roller coaster; they need someone who will listen and comfort them.

# DID YOU READ IT YET?

*Roberta G. Lojko*

"So Ms. Harris, did you read my paper yet?" The voice is eager, yet shy; a note of hope colors its expression. "You know, the paper I wrote yesterday." (Or the journal entry or the report.) "Did you get a chance to read it yet?"

I stood, stalled in corridor traffic, behind my fully laden cart. That's right, my cart. I am one of those itinerant teachers with no classroom of her own, who pushes around the tools of her trade on a cart, like some comic bag lady.

"Not yet, Mike, but I'll try to get to it tonight."

"Oh, OK." The voice is flat with disappointment.

And so I try, valiantly, to dig my way out of the essay avalanche and read each paper, respond with meaningful comments, and return each students' work sometime before they graduate. In the process it never ceases to amaze me how important their writing becomes to some students, how freely they reveal themselves to me and trust me with their most personal issues. Their writing becomes a window into their lives and personalities that they open innocently to let me see inside. I generally pride myself in responding to every student as quickly as I can, with interest and insight. But sometimes, there is that piece I should have read and responded to immediately, before it became too late to make a difference.

Dina had been in my English class for her first two years of high school, and I enjoyed her very much. She worked hard, wrote well, came to class prepared, and participated in positive ways. We had great rapport. One afternoon during journal writing she asked me to spell "Tylenol." I thought this was an odd request, but I did so obediently. The resident dictionary, I always spell out words for students rather than force them to pore over a dictionary for twenty minutes, trying to figure out why "psychology" does not appear under *s*.

After about ten minutes of writing, Dina walked quietly over to me, journal in hand. She placed it in front of me on the desk, open to the passage she had just written.

"Read this," she said simply.

I looked up, puzzled. "What do you want me to do with it afterwards?"

"Just read it," she said urgently, almost pleading.

Dutifully, I read. She had written about a girlfriend who had attempted suicide the day before by overdosing on pills. Dina was shocked and upset by her friend's actions but, more important, she felt tremendous guilt because she'd had no idea about the depth of her friend's despair.

She wrote, "I should have known. I'm a peer counselor and her best friend. I should have picked up on the clues. I should have known."

I looked up from the journal. Dina's dark blue eyes were soft pools of water.

"Dina, would you like to talk about this later?"

A nodded response.

"OK. Stay after class and we'll talk."

We spent an hour sitting in the empty classroom, confiding in each other, talking about how hard it is to be a teenager, to see one's friends in pain. We talked about the nature of suicide, what drives people to it, the act as a plea for help. I told Dina that she needed to absolve herself from feeling guilty, that her friend was responsible for her actions, no one else. By the end of the hour, I felt very close to Dina and very proud that she trusted me enough to ask for my help and comfort. That hour helped me believe in myself as a teacher. This was what working with kids was all about, being there for them when we can, as stable adults whom they can trust.

The winter months plodded wearily on. I was particularly pleased with the results of journal writing that year. I'd never been able to purchase enough blank books for all my students. Now both my freshman and my sophomore classes were writing in journals three times a week. I had mountains of journals to read at the end of each quarter. But I loaded them doggedly into brown shopping bags and read them at home, rather than abandon them or let students write without receiving any feedback. Released from the pressure of correctness, grading, and assigned topics, many students were doing their best writing in their journals. Confidentiality was essential, of course. The writer had control over who read the journal. Even my prying eyes were restricted at times.

The journal entries were windows on my students' lives beyond the classroom. This writing allowed me to make connections with kids that would not have happened otherwise. Sometimes my response to just one entry helped to create a link with a student where only indifference or disdain had existed before.

Around the second week in April, Dina didn't come to school. She was absent all that week and the next. A note from the guidance office requested assignments for her. I obliged, sending her journal along so she could keep up with her entries.

Toward the end of Dina's second week of absence, her guidance counselor called me in, just after lunch.

"I just wanted to let you know what's going on with Dina."

"Well, she's sick, isn't she? Did you get the assignments I handed in for her?"

"Yes, but I wanted to discuss the reason for her absence." She lowered her voice. What was she hiding? "Dina attempted suicide last week. She slashed her wrists. Fortunately, someone in her family found her in time. She's in the hospital psychiatric unit for observation and counseling."

I felt my throat and stomach tightening. How could she? Why? She was bright, pretty, talented, had lots of friends. No steady boyfriend, but so what? Wait, she had written something in her journal about a guy, much older than she, someone she seemed to care about. But the relationship had sounded unstable, not very good for her. My mind raced. What had she written about him?

". . . have any idea how she had been feeling lately?" The counselor again. "How has she been acting? I mean, what were your impressions of her behavior during the past few weeks?"

I described her glowingly: a lovely girl, an excellent student, though rather serious. Someone who tends to take others' problems to heart and try to solve them. I told the counselor of our discussion earlier in the year and Dina's feelings about her friend's suicide attempt.

"What about her journal? Did you get a sense from reading it that she might be depressed or upset?" Clearly, she had already read it and drawn her own conclusions. Her voice took on a clinical tone.

I was beginning to feel uncomfortable. "Look, I can show you twenty journals that indicate depression. Two days later the same student is feeling great. That's just the nature of adolescents. You can't really take every depression seriously."

"We do." That tone again. "Any time you realize that a student is seriously depressed, you need to let us know."

I carefully explained the premise behind journal writing, its confidentiality, the freedom to write anything, the fact that I only read entries at the end of each quarter, not on a daily basis. Still, I sensed that she was not satisfied. She seemed to be waiting for me to reveal something more.

I left her office to face two more classes, trying to sort through the shock, sadness, guilt, and frustration I felt. That weekend I tried to recover, assuring myself that Dina was all right after all. She was receiving medical and psychological help. With time and support, she'd get through this, I was sure. I'd have to be more insightful when I read students' journals from now on. That was clear.

Ten minutes into Tuesday morning's classes, the wall phone rang insistently. I answered it, sure it would be for some absent student or another teacher who taught in the room. The guidance director wanted to see me today, at my earliest convenience. The "issue" had to be settled by 10:00 A.M. It had to be something about Dina. I was not in the clear yet.

I walked to the guidance office after class and knocked on the director's door. She and Dina's counselor smiled, motioned for me to enter and sit down. They looked at me kindly, then at each other, unsure about how to begin. My defenses up, I waited for the inevitable.

"Well, maybe I'll begin," the counselor said, smiling politely. "When I got to school this morning, Dina's parents were here, waiting to see me. They are very angry about the journal, Nora, and want to know why no one told them how their daughter was feeling."

"We didn't even have our coats off. They were here, all upset, demanding to see us," chimed in the director.

The rest of their discussion had been heated. Two anxious and saddened parents were trying to find someone to bear the responsibility for their daughter's desperate act. To them the journal entries were solid evidence of her state of mind, and they were holding me responsible for the consequences. My stomach grew tighter as I was informed, diplomatically, of the gravity of the situation. Both women continued to probe into what I had known, when I had known it, and why I hadn't shared the information with anyone.

"You're not a trained counselor, Nora. This puts a great deal of pressure on you. You need to share these things with us, not take all the responsibility upon yourself," the counselor advised.

"Did you read these journals every day and write comments back to the kids?" the director asked.

"No," I said, trying to stay calm. "I told you before. I only read the journals at the end of each quarter."

"So," she said, like a detective who had found a valuable clue, "you hadn't read this before Dina's attempt."

"No, I hadn't," I said. "But isn't most of this irrelevant? I admit to a certain amount of responsibility here, but what's the point? What about Dina? What can we do for her now?"

They assured me that she was getting the best care and further recommended that I read a few books on teenage suicide so I could be better informed about the symptoms. There was one more request.

"Would you be willing to allow the journal to be used as a tool in Dina's therapy?" the director asked.

I couldn't believe it. "It seems to me that any authority I might have over who reads the journal has been ignored. Everyone's read it recently but me. I guess it's fine, if you think it will help Dina. But shouldn't *she* be asked about using her journal?"

"No, she isn't capable of making that decision right now," the counselor said, smiling. "We just wanted your consent." I now think I should have refused.

I left the office thoroughly shaken. I still had a whole day's worth of classes to teach.

I managed to do it, though on the verge of tears. I finally let go when I reached my car in the parking lot that afternoon. I felt hurt and guilty, but mostly I was angry. How dare anyone hold me responsible for what had happened to Dina! All I had done was give a troubled girl a place where she could express herself safely and openly. Why was she able to write about things to share with me that she couldn't tell her parents or counselor? Why didn't they give that some thought? I only saw Dina for five forty-minute periods each week. I had known her for just over two years. She had come in contact with two trained counselors weekly. And her parents had been with her every day for fifteen years. Where did their responsibility come into the picture?

I thought about all the news reports and magazine articles that find public education guilty for all the ills of youth, their violence, their laziness, their lack of values. The public schools aren't doing enough. Or we aren't doing it correctly. Or often or early enough. More and more, the schools had become society's scapegoats. That week, those social trends had become painfully real and utterly personal for me.

I struggled with my emotions for the rest of the week. I thought of staying home, avoiding school and the students entirely. But that would be a cop-out. I had to resolve some issues of my own. Journal writing was not just a simple method to encourage self-expression. This approach carried some heavy liabilities. I thought I had been handling my role as teacher-reader well by reading each page, responding with light comments, subtle advice, or suggestions for further entries. Should I read the entries more often? Make special notes about students who seemed consistently upset, angry, or depressed? Report those findings to counselors?

Or was the whole technique just too volatile? Maybe I should just abandon journal writing entirely. I could go back to teaching innocuous literature and offer safe topics for student essays that wouldn't be too provocative. That way I could keep my distance and remain ignorant of my students' private lives. After all, I "wasn't trained" in this area, as the counselor had so keenly observed.

I reread certain journals the following week. There were some students who seemed consistently troubled. Comments that indicated depression held much more impact for me now. I noted several names and went to counselors, informing them of my concern and begging them to keep the information confidential when they spoke to students.

"Just talk to them, see if they're OK. You don't have to let them know I talked to you." I was playing both sides of the issue, I knew. My actions made me uncomfortable, but I couldn't risk another situation like Dina's. I made notes of the names of the students and my meetings with their counselors, not trusting my memory to keep track of the details.

I thought of Dina often during the weeks that followed. I wondered how she was and decided to write to her. I had to let her know that I was concerned and explain that the release of the journal was meant to help her, not embarrass her. It took me two weeks to sit down and compose the letter. How could I explain what had happened? And even if I could explain, would Dina be able to forgive me?

Before I had a chance to mail the letter, Dina appeared in my class one morning. There was no advance notice from her doctors, parents, or counselor. She was simply there, calmly sitting at her desk, ready to get back into things. I wanted to give her the letter, but the classroom filled quickly with students. So I held onto it, wondering if I should give it to her at all. It was time for starting fresh after all, not looking back.

The end of the school year came on fast. I became caught up with term papers, final exams, and projects. I helped Dina get caught up with her classmates and watched her closely in class. She seemed completely returned to herself, though I sensed the palpable distance she placed between us.

While Dina and her classmates took their final exams, I collected their journals and read them at my desk. I opened Dina's. There was only one entry, written just after her return to school in early May:

"I don't write in school journals anymore. It's just a waste of time. I have my own journal at home where I can write my thoughts and no one else reads them. I'll never write in a school journal again. They're so lame."

My heart sank. I'd violated her trust. I had this coming. Sighing, I reread the entry. I wanted so much to talk to her, to try to explain what had happened. I thought a minute more, then responded from the heart.

"Dina, I understand your feelings about journal writing. Here is a letter I have been meaning to give to you. I hope it will explain my actions somehow. Have a lovely summer. Hope I see you next year. As ever, Ms. Harris."

I placed the small blue envelope in the journal and laid it on Dina's desk. She pushed it aside and continued to work on her exam.

When the bell sounded, Dina and the other students dashed out. Only a few more exams to go until summer would liberate all of us. Left behind, I collected the students' tattered work folders, covered with personal graffiti. I opened Dina's. The journal and the letter were gone.

# REFLECTIONS

**Nancy O'Malley:** The Michael poem originated out of my need to produce a work for the student anthology that is created every summer at the Writers' Workshop at UMass, Boston. I bring together fifty students from Boston schools to write in an intensive two-week seminar. I write along with the students, submit my piece, and also read it at the ceremony that culminates the workshop. I had writers' block, was sitting on my back porch on a Sunday night, found myself remembering Michael, and was suddenly flooded with grief for him. For his aloneness, his uniqueness (biracial, bisexual, no family, no permanent home, nothing to call his own). I was absolutely stunned at the level of grief I felt during and after writing it. A friend came by and found me sobbing. I had never let myself feel how deeply tragic Michael was.

When I read "Michael" at the reading I felt the audience weep a little along with me. My voice cracked and I was glad. Students need to see their teachers as deeply touched by people as they are. The piece haunts me a little. I want to be able to help the Michaels so much more than just to give him a book or take him to the ballet.

**Eugenia Nicholas:** My piece, "Silence Is No Longer Golden," was the result of thinking I did after a field trip to the White Mountains. The trip was exhausting because there were so many emotional issues to deal with and kids were remarkably open about their problems. I am more convinced than ever that we at the middle-school level must respond to students on an emotional level as well as an academic one. The problem is how to do this when working with ninety-plus children on a daily basis, how to do it with a schedule that moves students swiftly from one class to another and requires teachers and students to switch gears instantaneously.

**Roberta Lojko:** Writing about this experience crystallized for me the incredible power and fragility of the relationship between teachers of writing and their students. I pride myself on developing assignments that students can relate to personally and bring something of themselves to. However, the flip side of this approach is the responsibility we have as teachers to honor students' ideas and beliefs, keep their confidences for the most part, but share students' reactions if they seem to indicate intense personal problems or harmful behavior. It's a real tightrope I walk that I never understood until I had this experience. The most painful part of the piece for me is the destruction of the relationship between Nora and Dina, based on what Dina perceives as the violation of her trust by her teacher.

# V

# Acknowledging and Supporting the Diversity of All Learners (Including Teachers)

ortunately, one of the directions in which the field of education has aimed and, to a certain extent, moved is towards acknowledging diversity and supporting the talents and needs that recognition of diversity brings to school and society.

But change is difficult. It requires new learning. That doesn't happen without a catalyst, time, and support. While the realities of life in school frequently provide a catalyst, most teachers have so little time and support for change that their energies often go to the most compelling need they see, day by day, the content and methodology of what they teach. Sitting through the increasingly common two-hour workshop on diversity is not enough, for most teachers, to bring about the integration of broader understanding of social diversity into the curriculum. While it suits the professional and personal goals of some, it seems impossible, or irrelevant, to others.

In addition, teachers are often encouraged to focus their professional development on issues of curriculum and assessment. Increased awareness of varied learning styles has begun to address some aspects of the diversity of students. However, until recently, and excluding certain progressive pockets, considering issues surrounding diversity in ways beyond learning styles has generally been considered beyond the parameters of professional development.

Few teachers are bigots. Teachers teach because they care about school, children, and society. Teachers know they touch the future. How many have uttered the heartfelt words, "I'd do the right thing more often if I only knew what the right thing was"? In the case of diversity, it isn't just knowing right from wrong, which most teachers do know. It's recognition of identity. It's knowing a context. To most teachers, these are new determinants of appropriate roles, interrelationships, and interactions.

BEVERLY LUCEY lends some real faces to this need for greater familiarity.

*Now that we're getting more Asians and Hispanics in town and in the school, I have learned a few things on my own about some of the Hispanic boys. There is a tendency to be resistant to direct instruc-*

*tion, so I have to find other ways to give directions sometimes. I have to be careful not to look stern and "this is last straw"-ish. Most kids read this as "better back off from Lucey," but the few Hispanic boys seem to see this as more of a challenge. I am really guessing at all this, but that's how it seems to me. On the other hand, it seems that no Asian student ever shows temper or irritation. How can that be? We also get students who have attended nine years of an alternative school in town and have a delightful, kind, touchy-feely way about them. They seem bewildered by the pace and brusqueness of a school with a plethora of rules that do not seem to respect their individuality.*

*In some ways, things are improving. [For example,] more than six years ago a young man assumed to be gay was physically harassed out of school . . . it was an awful period of time. Any discussion about gay rights was very difficult to field in a class. Within the last two years the students seem a bit more open to respect for diversity, and a few weeks ago, for the very first time in my career, a female student came out in class.*

Increased racial, ethnic, and social diversity in school has created greater pressure to recognize and support diversity. While the greatest challenge has been ignorance, resistant attitudes and behaviors have also been invisible barriers. Those unyielding attitudes are reminiscent of a line from the popular movie of a few years ago, *Field of Dreams*. In that movie, the voice said, "If you build it, they will come." The unspoken motto in many schools for too long has been, "If they come, we will deal with it."

While the contributors to this book have come to their conceptual frameworks from several directions, they are united in and by their assumption of the great richness availed by diversity.

A sense of hope and belief in the highest of democratic ideals influences their assumptions about teaching.

AMY MANN: *At the bottom of it all . . . I believe all students can learn. I believe in equity and equal access to knowledge. I believe that schools, communities of learning, can change the world.*

DAVID SUMMERGRAD: *I am particularly conscious of the criticisms of public schools today and the rise of an entrepreneurial private school movement. . . . It is easy to claim that you can "do education better" if you don't have to teach all the students who show up at your doorstep, but what makes American public education so special is the fact that it is so deeply rooted in essential democracy—free compulsory public education for all.*

Others give credit to inspiration from those they have studied.

JANE KATCH: *My professional career began as a counselor working with severely emotionally disturbed children at a residential treatment center run by Bruno Bettelheim. I learned from him that it is possible to understand anyone, no matter how strange the person's behavior seems, by first understanding myself.*

DANIEL MURPHY: *Years ago I read many books that influenced me deeply. One of them,* The Art of Loving *by Erich Fromm, comes immediately to mind. Fromm wrote about love as being mutual caring, respect, knowledge, and responsibility. This perspective is one I feel viscerally. I love my students, their diverse backgrounds, and their unique personal qualities. I am grateful to them for teaching me so much.*

Their own identities and family backgrounds have informed their teaching.

RIC CALLEJA: *My experience as a twelve-year-old immigrant in Boston made me keenly aware of human differences and similarities, the challenge to find common ground with those whom I come into contact with. The many misunderstandings, generalizations, and stereotypes that I encountered growing up about Spanish-speaking people and the countries we come from motivated me to teach the Spanish language, and to help students understand the cultures and peoples of the Spanish-speaking world.*

LINDA FERNSTEN: *My own father spoke English as a second language, but in his day there were no ESL classes and little understanding of "foreign" language speakers, much less appreciation. He told me how teachers used to ridicule his French accent and how he grew to hate school and mistrust teachers. I knew the kind of teacher I didn't want to be—I knew the tale I wanted my students to be able to tell their children. In every child who feels different, an outsider stuck in the system, I see my father.*

Teaching is a "people profession." Reflection on the role of interpersonal dynamics as part of the content as well as the process of education can provide direction.

DIANE DANTHONY: *Although we like to think so, teaching is not primarily about content. It's really about relationships—students with students, teacher with students, and, finally, teacher and students with content. Respecting and supporting diversity is all about relationships—observing, enjoying, and learning from the differences and samenesses of students and what they bring to the learning process, and to the content. Bottom line: it means opening my heart, sharing, listening, and accepting without judging.*

Finally, BEVERLY LUCEY suggests that being a writer, with a writer's need to observe and question, sharpens her appreciation of individuals.

*Being a teacher who writes [has meant that] it isn't the groups or cliques that are the focus of my concern, it's the uniqueness of so many individuals' lives. How do I capture, hold, nurture, honor and let go?*

With the basic assumption of kinship and a resulting insistence on equity underpinning their approach to teaching, each contributor has developed certain practices that have increased the inclusiveness, accessibility, and effectiveness of the teaching and learning in their classrooms. These practices range from ways of being and practice of critical pedagogy to the school environment and classroom structures and programs.

Knowing that students learn more from what teachers do than from what they say, AMY MANN offers a pathway toward equity:

*Include students in decision-making [and] have high expectations for student achievement, heterogeneous grouping, a student-centered, discussion-based classroom and curriculum.*

Contributors note the key role that modeling plays in their teaching and in their strategic approach to the creation of effective learning environments. No matter the subject matter or the age of the students, this "curriculum," more or less spoken, is seen as essential.

EUGENIA NICHOLAS: *I create a warm and welcoming place with plants, posters, students' work displayed with pride. The classroom management is more a way of being with others than a list of rules. I treat students with respect. I listen to them. . . . I insist they listen to each other, grant each other the right to speak, and allow each other to learn at their own rates. This is accomplished with consistent training, and on any given day we may have a breakthrough or a setback. Whichever the case may be, we continue trying and working at the model of mutual respect, mutual giving, and mutual caring.*

TESS BOYLE: *I try to be alert for teachable moments and have zero tolerance for racial remarks. I try to create a place where it is safe to be whoever you are.*

NANCY ALLEN: *Creating an atmosphere of trust and openness where questions can be asked and risks can be taken is most important in establishing an anti-bias classroom. Teachers must model frequently in different situations how they value diversity. . . . Assessment samples should be looked at for what the child can do and is attempting to do in order to promote self-esteem. The child will see him- or herself with unique strengths and be more able to accept weaknesses.*

DIANE DANTHONY: *Students are dealing with some very difficult circumstances. [I know we must] take care of first things first . . . make some room for honest personal discussion. I believe this is the only way we can succeed individually and as a group, and then eventually approach our academic goals.*

Building on these ways of being by increasing students' knowledge and awareness of culture(s) is central to their teaching.

DAVID SUMMERGRAD: *Make sure that students see themselves in what you include in the curriculum and what you put on the walls.*

RIC CALLEJA: *Students who understand their own cultural backgrounds and explore and celebrate other cultures will be better prepared to live and work with others who see the world through different cultural lenses.*

NANCY O'MALLEY: *It is essential to create an atmosphere where every individual voice is listened to. That is an absolute. I spend time in my English and writing classes establishing the rules that every voice will be heard. . . . Let students tell their family stories and histories and allow them to be valued by other students. . . . Students read aloud from a journal excerpt or a work in progress. . . . In a similar vein, I insist on hearing the words of famous [Latino, African, Asian, Native, and European American] writers who can inspire us all. . . . I ask students to keep detailed notebooks that contain facts about famous authors' lives, and they discover for themselves the powerful words and ideas in the books, poems, plays [and each other's writing]. . . . That means each student compiles a series of quotes from the work of each other. The quotes are powerful sentences and word choices that the student values.*

BEVERLY LUCEY: *I do a lot of [work with] point of view and what affects it, both in literature and in the world around us, often talking about how the characters become who they are. I try to reinforce the idea that different is not weird or bad or wrong. I show multicultural films,* The Great Wall, El Norte, The Gods Must Be Crazy. *I question, explore, and try to debunk stereotypes, discuss racial, ethnic, and sexist jokes. I admit to being a part of the problem and not having all the answers. One of my room rules is no insults. Sometimes I have to let them know what insults are, they are so used to doing it—or ignorant about what terms are not OK.*

SUSANNE RUBENSTEIN: *In an English classroom there are many opportunities to examine and applaud the differences that exist among people. Literature is full of heroes who struggle to maintain their individuality in a world that would like them to conform. . . . We can find individuals who don't quite fit, but who are richer, more interesting people because of it. The discussions students have about these fictional characters allow them to explore their own questions and concerns, their prejudices and presumptions in a safe environment. Such discussions, too, often serve as a springboard for students' own writing. In my classroom, much of my students' writing focuses on two questions: Who am I? How do I fit into the world? The thoughts they share—in response groups, in papers tacked to the wall, in public readings—open the door to differences.*

An essential ingredient of effective, inclusive classrooms is trust, which is often difficult to establish, especially at higher grades. In addition to the practices described above, sharing one's own experience and participating in the assignments along with the students can contribute in ways nothing else does. More and more teachers do this as part of writing instruction. To accomplish that and avoid self-indulgence, not to mention downright boredom among students, this should be done with insight and good sense. That criterion met, when a teacher is comfortable doing so, the modeling can have value, in terms of building trust as well as in illuminating the process of composing writing from experience.

ROBERTA LOJKO: *I write most of the major pieces with the students and share my writing with them to offer them a window into my personality and inner life. If I am not afraid to open myself to them through my writing, I can generally allay their anxiety about doing the same.*

Ultimately, good teaching is good teaching, and school structures and programs enhance or impede it.

DIANA CALLAHAN: *Cooperative learning and the multi-age classroom concept have been the most helpful to me. When children are sur-*

*rounded by peer-models and immersed in literacy activities at many different entry levels, they are more likely to succeed. . . . The increased diversity in a multi-age classroom leads to greater acceptance of individual difference as well as increased opportunity to group according to individual need and interest. Children work together and view differences as not a characteristic of ability but rather just what an individual is learning or working on at the time. There really is no expectation that everyone should be at the same place at the same time.*

As stand-alone, one-time events, specific programs have little impact, but as part of the more comprehensive teaching toward diversity articulated by these teachers, special events, organizations, and units build interest and knowledge.

TESS BOYLE: *We share ethnic foods as early in the year as possible. Nothing captures everyone's interest the way food does. It also is a chance for parents to come to school. Another thing I do is a project on movement (immigration). I plan it so students can interview relatives over the Thanksgiving vacation and tell stories when they come back to school.*

BEVERLY LUCEY: *We have a student group that has been concerned about issues of racism, sexism, and homophobia. For the last two years we have suspended classes and had an annual day-long harmony festival at school, [with] concerts, speakers, special T-shirts, an outdoor barbeque, noncompetitive games, and serious softball between faculty and students.*

Behind everything rests the knowledge that despite (or within) the layers of uniqueness or diversity, we all share a kinship, whether of similarity, recognition, or empathy.

# VI

# Organizing and Conducting a Writers' Retreat for Teachers

A three-day conference, no matter how wonderful, will not make a writer out of anyone. It can inspire and give the mental and emotional space for starting some powerful writing. It can be a memorable experience, full of the euphoria and pathos that come from sustained, deep thought and shared reflections on teaching and living. It can engender the commitment to find more opportunities to write or develop more disciplined writing habits. All these possibilities (and more) are considered in the planning of the Center's writers' conference—how to do the best with the time we have.

More broadly stated, the retreat is based on the Center's own goals of providing opportunities for reflective teaching practice and building the inclusion of practitioner knowledge—teachers' own voices—into conversations on education. To that end, there are three elements of focus in the planning of the writers' retreats: people, program, and location.

# PEOPLE

It takes four types of people to make the writers' retreat successful: participants who register to attend, writing group facilitators engaged to lead and participate in the writing groups, guest speakers, and the conference coordinator.

## Participants

The participants who register to attend the writers' retreats come from all over the state and teach at every level, prekindergarten through college. Some have never written more than they needed to get by. Others write and publish routinely. Most fall into every conceivable category between.

Some arrive quivering with fear. Who can say what makes them come? Often they register from a sense of need, feeling they should improve their own writing if they expect their students to write, or if they are to improve their teaching of writing. All leave surer of themselves as writers, some having written and shared their writing for the first time, others having become rejuvenated. Some of the more experienced and confident writers bring work to start, develop, or complete. Others come knowing they'll leave with an idea, a fresh perspective, a start.

# Writing Group Facilitators

Writing group facilitators are central to the success of the retreat. They are classroom teachers and teacher educators who have substantial experience as teachers. Many have close connections with the National Writing Project and carry with them the concomitant respect for teachers, the value of reflection and writing, and the staying power of learning by doing.

They help shape the schedule within which they plan and implement the sessions that are the main body of the retreat. Most plan a succession of guided invitations to participants to reflect on, write, and share significant teaching and learning situations. While this generally raises images of classrooms, the sessions are not necessarily meant to be connected to school life. The idea is for participants to remember a moment that has contributed to their identity in significant ways, often one that defines who they are as a person and a teacher.

Participants in writers' retreats need and deserve facilitators who can provide them with cognitive, procedural, and even emotional scaffolding. Facilitators must be both attuned to the participants and steeped in exemplary writing practice. (A book that the facilitators are sure to have read, one that informs the approach to writing that permeates the writers' retreat, is *Writing with Power* by Peter Elbow.)

But along with the metacognitive potential of reflection and writing, which serves as a lens through which to re-view (or view from a different perspective) the subject of reflection, comes the discovery of mysterious terrain. Writing can elicit vulnerabilities that were previously unacknowledged. Most people need to be made aware of useful (as opposed to hurtful or unproductive) ways to respond to others' writing, not to mention their own.

Facilitators must be a hardy crew, with skins of a certain thickness. They must be good at all the things that make a good teacher: they must know their subject area; they must plan well, but be flexible; they must be skilled at easing the writer's insecurities; they must know how to acknowledge the disquieting effects of the writing on both the writer and the audience; and they must be able just to listen and offer good suggestions.

# Guest Speakers

Early in the retreat, but after participants have had the chance to meet each other and write in their writing groups, a keynote speaker delivers an address. The keynote speaker is usually a teacher who writes and has achieved some significant success (generally publication) with her or his writing. Often a reading from the published work (which once included a cappella singing) is a highlight of the keynote address. That the keynote speaker be a teacher matters, considering the empathy and validation that can thus be shared between the speaker and the audience. Participants draw encouragement and inspiration from these presentations, which spur participants' own reflections and help set the tone of sincere absorption in the real work of writing.

To counteract the tension, isolation, and sameness that can result from long periods of time spent writing, the writers' retreat schedules a session midway through the retreat in which participants can choose to listen to a speaker, join in a discussion, take a walk, or even keep writing if that's what they choose to do.

During this session, at which attendance is optional, guest speakers have contributed to the mix of activities in a variety of ways. Some have lectured on writing. Others have contributed to panel discussions on topics related to writing and publishing: finding time to write, organizing or participating in writing groups, considering the how-tos of teaching, writing, and getting published. Editors from professional journals have explained manuscript requirements for submission, provided samples of their publications, and suggested ways to identify appropriate outlets for writing and how to market writing effectively.

# The Conference Coordinator

The conference coordinator orchestrates the site and activity arrangements, engages the facilitators, secures the keynote speaker, composes the schedule, and makes sure each detail works with all the others to produce three intricately textured days that build on each other. We have found it best for the conference coordinator not to participate in a writing group, but rather to remain constantly accessible to all. Even with the best-made plans, of course, there are always unanticipated problems—such as, for example, a light sleeper paired with someone who snores or likes to write through the night. In such cases, room arrangements must be altered on the spot, details best attended to while the writing groups are in session. The conference coordinator's goal is always to resolve issues in ways that are least distracting to the participants, who are there to write.

A good conference coordinator must have clear insight into the goals of the retreat, respect for the nature of the participants' work, knowledge of how to support what that work entails, organizational skills, and the ability to recognize and satisfy reasonable requests from the participants and facilitators. It is also important that the coordinator be assertive, be able to get or accomplish what is needed, take initiative, make decisions regarding unforeseen situations, and be unflappable. The Center has generally turned to one of the directors or someone intimately involved with the Center's work to serve as the conference coordinator.

# PROGRAM

The program of the writers' retreat is informed by sound pedagogy. Time is structured to provide participants with the opportunity to generate, explore, practice, and receive response to writing. Attention to the variety of processes involved in writing is central, as is sensitivity to varying comfort levels and varying levels of achievement. In addition, knowledge that learning by doing is essential for adults (as for all learners) prompts facilitators to limit lecturing in favor of inviting the participants into writing.

The retreat opens with an introductory session designed to acquaint the participants with one another, to set a collegial tone, and to establish the empowering goals. Participants then share a meal and move into writing groups. Participants spend most of their time within one of seven writing groups.

Five writing groups make up the core of the program. In them, participants and the writing group facilitator generate, explore, experiment with, and experience the potential and power of writing within the support of a group. Two smaller groups, called response groups, focus on intensive feedback for the participants, all of whom enter the groups with works in progress. While response to writing occurs in all groups, response groups are concerned primarily with response and revision. Participants seeking to concentrate on feedback sign up accordingly on the conference registration form.

The real work of the retreat takes place in several writing sessions, each two to four hours long, primarily in groups. The specific number and duration of the writing sessions have varied over the years, but the aim is to carve out as many blocks of time as possible. During long, uninterrupted writing periods, some participants opt to write in their rooms, returning at prearranged times for interactions with the group.

The schedule for the most recent retreat was as follows:

Day 1:    11:00 A.M.–noon        Welcome/Introductions
            noon–1:00 P.M.          Lunch

|        | 1:15–4:00 P.M.          | Writing groups                                          |
|--------|-------------------------|--------------------------------------------------------|
|        | 5:00–6:00 P.M.          | Keynote address                                        |
|        | 6:15–7:30 P.M.          | Dinner                                                 |
|        | 7:45–9:45 P.M.          | Writing groups                                         |
| Day 2: | 8:30 A.M.–noon          | Writing groups                                         |
|        | 12:15–1:15 P.M.         | Lunch                                                  |
|        | 1:30–3:00 P.M.          | Panel discussion or other activity                     |
|        | 3:15–5:30 P.M.          | Writing groups                                         |
|        | 7:00–9:00 P.M.          | Dinner and readings by annual writers' contest winners |
| Day 3: | 8:30–11:30 A.M.         | Writing groups                                         |
|        | 11:45 A.M.–12:45 P.M.   | Celebratory reading                                    |

Within the core writing groups, participants move from community building through longer and more demanding and complex invitations to write, share, respond to, and ultimately revise their writing. In the two response groups, community building is followed by the recursive process of response, reflection, revision, response, and so on.

Although the groups are similar in vision and approach, the details of the "life" of each writing group varies with the style, personality, and priorities of the facilitator and with the dynamics of the group. Some writing group facilitators participate fully in the activities they have devised for the other members of the group. Others set things in motion, oversee, and provide support, but do not do the activities themselves.

One facilitator's plan for the most recent writers' retreat is provided in the appendix. It is just one of many possibilities, and is not intended to be used so much as a model as simply to demystify the planning process. As stated earlier, each facilitator approaches the three days differently. Some use a complex, sequential plan; others try a more fluid approach, in order to respond to the rhythm of the group and the needs of the participants as the retreat unfolds. The plan in the appendix shows what one facilitator was comfortable doing one year. Participants moved through the scheme eagerly and engaged in the activities fully, showing evidence of serious thought, a sense of discovery, and feelings of satisfaction; and they gave the retreat a positive evaluation.

With each succeeding year, more retreat participants return, frequently with a colleague. While the Center's retreats take place in early December, repeat participants often make arrangements early in the academic year (when school budgets are more likely to support professional development) with their school administrators to attend. Some ask for it as a gift. Some give it to themselves. This growing body of returnees is both a resource and a challenge. They are a resource in that they are already acquainted with the overall goals of the retreat, have assimilated many of the writing attitudes and practices and are comfortable with them, and manifest an obvious love for the retreat experience. They are invaluable role models for those attending for the first time and a great support and joy to each other.

It is a challenge both to integrate returnees with new participants and to ensure that the retreat provides returnees with new perspectives and satisfying experiences. One strategy is to place returnees as much as possible into writing groups with facilitators and participants other than those they were with in previous retreats. This is done by examining records from the prior retreat and assigning groups accordingly.

Another way we have responded to the influx of returning participants is by instituting the response groups mentioned earlier. In fact, response groups are the result of participants' requests for help developing pieces begun a year earlier into publishable condition. Participants who select "response group" on the conference registration form are instructed to submit a manuscript that is in progress. What we do with those manuscripts may vary as we develop the concept. Last year, the first with response groups, we made enough copies for all the members of the group and sent the bundle to the facilitator to read in preparation for the retreat and distribute to the other group members during the first session. Another year we might send copies of manuscripts in advance to all the group members. Last year we limited the length of the manuscripts to five pages; we might reconsider that in the future. Facilitators know best what they can manage within the groups.

The five core groups at the retreat are composed to bring together the full range of diversity of the participants. This means that in a given group there may be teachers from different geographic areas (rural, urban, suburban) and from different disciplines and grade levels. They may have varying experience with writing; they may be first-time or repeat participants. Our knowledge of most participants is limited to information on the registration forms (gender, geographic area, and teaching assignment), but we do know a bit more about repeat conference participants and teachers who have participated in other Field Center programs. This knowledge helps us aim toward heterogeneity in the writing groups.

We have weighed the relative advantages of homogeneous groups, rather than mixed groups. There is something to say for grouping people from the same geographic area. That might encourage their setting up writing groups to meet throughout the year near their homes. (This has happened despite not grouping by proximity.) There may also be something to gain in grouping by grade level, where participants would immediately find common experiences. Grouping writers according to their level of experience with writing might stimulate experienced writers to higher achievement and make inexperienced writers feel more secure.

Ultimately, our approach to grouping, while partly a guessing game and to some extent random, is based on the principle that grouping by categories limits possibilities and the richness of experience. People are so much more than any category they might fall into. Year after year, we see evidence of this in the stimulating mix of powerful writing— poetry, essay, fiction, personal narrative—as well as the strong bonds, the appreciation, and the recognition of commonalities that result from the heterogeneous groups. The richness of this variety would have been diluted in groups defined by geography or experience.

Not inconsequently, participants, especially repeat participants, employ processes practiced at the retreats in their own classrooms. They mention such practices as increasingly skilled use of open questions, guided invitations to write (rather than merely assigning writing), the sharing of their own writing with students, and more learner-centeredness in their classrooms—all modeled by facilitators and experienced by the retreat participants. This lends validity to the notion that the learning, practice, and reflection teachers experience at writers' retreats directly benefit their students.

# LOCATION

Certainly, writing groups can function smoothly and efficiently in a classroom, a library, or any available place when the will is present. Our insistence on a top-notch site, away from school, is to honor the whole person, not only the teacher, in the teachers and to bring them from their daily world into a place that offers them a different perspective on that daily world.

As a group, teachers rarely gather and work in seaside or mountain resorts, with gourmet meals to delight their palates and great attention paid to their creature comforts. That is precisely our aim in choosing a location for the writers' retreats: to stimulate and pamper the participants. The care the participants receive is noted and much appreciated.

We choose a fine hotel or inn with a comfortable work space for each writing group. Participants most often share rooms, which we assign. The pleasure and serenity drawn from the charming accommodations spill over into the performance of the participants. Treated so well, they work eagerly.

Mealtimes are celebrations of their own. The food is for more than physical sustenance. Meals are the bookends to the daily writing sessions, a respite from the often grueling mental work of writing.

A mountain, a beach, a quiet place for solitary reflection—all are good sites for a writers' retreat. Not all writing is done sitting with pen and paper. At times, there is more to be gained from quiet time spent outdoors, alone. Serenity of place can open the way for clarifying thinking, can help breathe order or meaning into an otherwise impenetrable jumble of thoughts or impressions.

While the focus on place might sound like making much of the insignificant, such details contribute to the overall experience of the writers' retreats. It's amazing how often we hear gratitude expressed for the linen, the china, the ocean views, and the service. This is stark evidence of how little teachers expect for themselves and how rarely they experience niceties in their work lives. All the more reason to provide them.

# APPENDIX

## Writing Group Facilitator's Sample Plan

This appendix presents a plan that was used for facilitating a writing group. Scattered throughout are abbreviated scripts, shown in parentheses, which are meant to serve as prompts. The plan starts with short activities and considerable directiveness. As it progresses, there are fewer directions, longer work periods, and more opportunities for participants to direct their own use of time and effort. Occasionally, handouts or pieces of literature are distributed. The handouts, which vary from year to year, serve to channel thoughts, memories, and writing. Much of the material in this plan has been gathered from other sources, which the facilitator has combined and adapted to suit her own goals and personal style.

This plan is not intended as a model; it is a *sample,* just one possible approach to facilitating a writing group.

# FIRST SESSION

1. Unclogging—free writing. *(To help us all focus—to flush out the day, the trip, the confusion. Just spend the next ten or so minutes writing whatever comes to mind or is on your mind—private, not to be shared—before we move to introductions.)*

2. Introductions. We read together a short piece of writing, this year, "My Name is Esperanza" from *The House on Mango Street* by Sandra Cisneros. *(Write in any way about any or all of your names—what you are called, call yourself—to be shared.)* We use bits of our stories to introduce ourselves to one another.

3. Warm-up/writing spurts. To generate a discussion on the challenges involved in writing, to get our fears and anxieties about writing out in the open and thus to defuse them, I ask that people look into their past or the present to moments that have shaped their attitudes and experiences with writing. We do some listing and sharing. There are no right answers. I ask just for first

thoughts. Volunteers read their notes of some of those moments. I summarize, noting differences and similarities. Then, having acknowledged that we all dread some things about writing, we leave the subject.

4.  A few words about my goals and the process here, as I envision it. (This is my longest lecture.)

*Goals:*

❖ both private and shared writing
❖ both prompted and self-directed writing
❖ writing both together and independently
❖ reflecting/writing on professional and personal experiences
❖ time to finish and even polish a piece
❖ time to start several pieces to pick up later

*Process:*

❖ thinking, talking, writing, reading, listening
❖ increasingly longer periods of writing time
❖ varied opportunities and strategies for writing, response, and revision
❖ increasingly larger audiences (*I'll ask you to share much of what you've written, but you are free not to.*)
❖ choice (*I'll make suggestions, but they are optional and should be disregarded if something else takes priority in your thinking.*)
❖ opportunity for a blend of support and autonomy (*If you have a particular pressing writing goal, use your time for that, as long as you can continue to enter into sharing time with the rest of the group. Tell me if you need time on your own, so I can let you know when to re-enter into the group.*)
❖ variety of genres, all equally suitable (*Poetry, if that's how you think; essay, formal or informal; story/narrative—you choose what suits you best.*)

5. We use the rest of the session, in forty-five-minute chunks, to start a couple of drafts. We save sharing for the evening session when people are too full from dinner and too tired from writing to write any more. In addition, waiting until evening to share provides people with more time to get to know one another. *(For now, give yourselves a few moments to see an image of yourself in a classroom, either as student or teacher, that you have over and over again—maybe a vivid memory. List in words and/or short phrases one or two lines long as many images as you can in either category, student or teacher. The only requirement is that the memories or images have a strong visual or auditory component or a strong emotional impact for you. List as many as you can in the next few minutes.)*

   I then ask people to rank their entries, with 1 being the most powerful and/or frequently sensed. Volunteers share their first entry. Then we go around again for the second, the third, and so on, so that participants can hear what others are doing. Then we write for approximately thirty minutes (I keep track of time) from whatever image or memory that has taken hold. This writing sometimes takes the form of a personal narrative or description. It may have the sound or feel of a story, or just be strings of images, thoughts, and feelings. *(You should aim to be writing freely, making a messy draft. Don't look for craft as much as for feeling, thinking, and self-expression.)*

6. After a short break, we start another piece, but first we read something short and inspiring that affirms both the uniqueness and universality of individuals. This year, we read "Giants, Wizards and Dwarfs" from *All I Need to Know I Learned in Kindergarten* by Robert Fulghum. *(Take a few minutes to hear what stands out to you, either from the perspective of the child or the adult. Think about the center of its meaning for you—a message you pull out of it.)* We write for about thirty minutes on reactions/connections to this piece.

7. Summarize/debrief. Having begun several pieces of writing during this first session, we'll be given time to reflect on them and read and hear some during the second session.

# SECOND SESSION

1. I ask people to take a few minutes and reflect, in writing, on the process they've gone through so far, pretending they were looking over their own shoulder. This will be shared writing.

2. *(Ground rules during sharing in the whole group: just as in the classroom, remember how scary it can be to speak up in a group and share your work. Some of us may feel comfortable, but some will feel anxious and uncertain. Be sensitive to how your gestures and comments may be interpreted. For example, smiles, grunts, nods, and moans may be fine, but snorts might be interpreted as derision.)*

3. For the rest of the session, we use the following procedure. *(First, privately review whichever piece you will read for the group. If you don't want to read the entire piece, bracket the parts you plan to share, to make it easier for you to see what's in and what's out while you're reading. Begin your reading with your reflection on the process of the writing you just did. Then read the actual piece. Try to just read it through, without explanation or apology. All our writing is rough and tentative at this point.)* I ask for volunteers.

   While we listen, I ask that people jot down words or phrases that stand out to them for whatever reason. After each reader is done, I ask for a few volunteers to read what they noted back to the author. That's the only form of feedback we do the first night. I make sure everyone has had a chance to be heard. When we've finished, I summarize the comments, noting patterns, differences, effects of prompts, and so forth.

4.    Looking ahead. *(Tomorrow, there will be more suggestions for writing, as well as time to write, respond in small groups, and try some poetry.)*

# THIRD SESSION

The third session is broken into three one-hour writing exercises. Time for response in small groups is provided in the fourth session.

1.    The photo album exercise. This exercise encourages participants to do some creative imaging. They compose a list of photographs from their childhood that "jump off the page" at them, that spark strong feelings, memories, questions, or responses of any kind. From that list, participants choose one or two from which to write.

2.    A poetry exercise. This year I used an idea from an article, "Ten Untrue Statements about . . . " by Tom Murphy in *English Journal* (February 1989). I asked participants to list untrue statements about the moon. We each wrote one such statement—a huge lie or a mere inaccuracy or misunderstanding—on each of ten index cards. Then I collected the cards, shuffled them, and read them back to the group. This produced sighs, moans, and laughter. Then I scattered the cards onto a centrally located table, suggesting that people look through them and pick one or more to work from in any way that comes to them, keeping in mind (if possible) that they are striving for some kind of poetic expression. We don't get too serious about poetic form, but this kind of exercise, especially on the topic of something as evocative and elemental as the moon, just begs to become poetry. My intention is to break down the anxiety many of us face when we contemplate writing poetry—or teaching it.

Another time I brought a chocolate box full of words cut from magazines. Each person takes a small handful, spending some time gleaning the "good" ones, sifting them into lines. Eventually something of interest results from the process. It's magical. (I've seen some magnetic kits in recent years that are much more polished than my old chocolate box, not to mention less time-consuming to acquire.)

3.    Then we read something short that will dig into the recesses of people's hearts. This is intended to engage people in an intense and personal way. Since they have several pieces started and they only need to choose one of them to share, it gives them permission to write something they might keep private. People often share this piece, but the knowledge that they won't need to keeps the censor in them at bay. This year we read Robert Fulghum's "Hide and Seek" from *All I Need to Know I Learned in Kindergarten.* I ask people to *(think of some way in which you have been hidden and write from that thought).*

# FOURTH SESSION

1.    We use the first two hours of the fourth session to do a bit of preliminary self-editing, then read and respond in groups of three. I ask people to choose one piece, reread it, considering any or all of the following reader-based, nonevaluative questions. *(What seems to hold the piece together? Where is its conceptual or emotional center? Is there anything still unsaid? Anything you think a reader would want or need to hear more about? What's lurking? Are there any places that might be put more in the background? or more in the foreground?)*

This session has two purposes. One is for each writer to get a perspective on his or her draft by reading it aloud. A second is for each writer to hear how two listeners experience the draft. There is time during unassigned periods and during the final session to incorporate some of the writers' own thinking and the responses from their partners into the piece they work on. One writer reads; the others listen carefully and take notes as necessary. The writer may need to read his or her draft twice. Then the listeners discuss their responses before moving on to the next writer's piece. I ask that each group figure out a way to divide the time fairly among the readers.

2.  Debriefing. The assumption is that people have some ideas on where to take one or more of their pieces and that they'll take some time at least to sketch in for themselves what some of those ideas are. There will be time for sharing some piece of writing in a more developed draft form with the whole writing group during the final session.

# FIFTH SESSION

1.  By now we've had time to start several drafts, to reflect, write, and get feedback. *(During this last session, there will be some time to revise and develop your piece both from the feedback you've received and your own progression of thinking, so that eventually you can bring the piece to a larger audience: our group, then maybe a larger audience—the whole retreat or people back home or at school. You might even decide to submit the piece for publication somewhere—the local paper as an opinion or local-interest piece or a "Letter to the Editor," a school publication, a professional journal, whatever.)*

2.  I invite people to use the first ninety minutes of this session in the way that is most useful to them. That varies because people have done varying amounts of work, some independently. They

might work on revising the piece they got responses on during the previous session. They might, if they find others interested in doing the same, get feedback on something they've not yet shared. They might work on something they've just started with which they want more time.

3.  When we reconvene I ask people to say in advance what kind of response they would like. We listen with a purpose if the writer wants us to, after which a couple of people can volunteer their responses.

    By this time, we have become allies, and few of us hesitate to share the most powerful piece we've written.

# CONTRIBUTORS

*(All schools listed are in Massachusetts unless otherwise noted.)*

Nancy Allen was a Chapter I reading and writing specialist for many years in the Northampton School district. She is currently co-teaching third grade and mentoring colleagues in The Learning Network's literacy learning model, as well as planning for an upcoming trip to China to bring back her adopted daughter.

Tess Boyle is a sixth-grade social studies teacher at Kiley Middle School in Springfield. She enjoys writing about her students.

Diana Callahan is a primary level multi-age classroom teacher and staff mentor in Easthampton, Massachusetts. She currently serves as one of the co-directors of the Western Massachusetts Writing Project, where she is responsible for organizing response groups for teachers who write.

Ricardo Calleja teaches Spanish at Brookline High School. He is a member of the Field Center's Editorial Advisory Committee and participates in a weekly writing group.

diane danthony is an English teacher at Minnechaug Regional High School in Wilbraham, Massachusetts. She is also an educational consultant, providing training in classroom management and creating effective work groups.

Cathie (Spence) Desjardins co-directs the HEART (Home Enrichment and Reading Team) Program, a parent-home reading project which works with the Boston Public Schools. Based at the Institute for Learning and Teaching at the University of Massachusetts Boston, she teaches there in the Graduate College of Education.

Linda Fernsten teaches high school English in South Deerfield, Massachusetts. She is currently working on a doctorate at the University of Massachusetts, Amherst. She is a member of the Western Massachusetts Writing Project and has spent the last two summers teaching in a post-secondary school in Europe.

John Hodgen is a teacher of Advanced Placement English and Creative Writing at Shrewsbury High School.

Jane Katch teaches children who are five, six, seven years old in a multi-age class at the Touchstone Community School in Grafton, Massachusetts.

E. J. Miller Laino is a prevention educator at Reading Memorial High School. She has published poems in journals and anthologies. Her first book of poetry, *Girl Hurt,* was published in 1995.

Joel B. Levine is a Licensed Educational Psychologist with the Hampshire Educational Collaborative in Northampton (MA). With co-author SiriNam Khalsa he wrote *Talking on Purpose: Practical Skill Development for Effective Communication.*

Roberta G. Lojko, a former high school English teacher, has recently become an assistant principal at Wachusett Regional High School in Holden, Massachusetts.

Beverly C. Lucey has been teaching English and Theater for close to thirty years at Greenfield High School in western Massachusetts. She has had stories published in *Portland Magazine, Aim,* and included in an anthology from Pineapple Press. She has twice won prizes for writing from the Massachusetts Field Center for Teaching and Learning.

Amy Mann is an English teacher at Guilderland High School (NY), where her work focuses on co-operative learning and the exploration of literature through personal and expository writing.

Daniel P. Murphy is a teacher at Lowell High School and a licensed family therapist. His poems have appeared in several journals, such as *Bitterroot, International Poetry Journal, Keltic Fringe,* and *Parnassus Literary Journal.* He also has published a book of poems, *The Fractured Emerald.*

Eugenia M. Nicholas has been a teacher, guidance counselor, assistant principal and principal. She is currently turning her thoughts to a new career which combines writing and healing.

Nancy O'Malley teaches English and writing at Boston Latin School. She also directs the Writers' Workshop at the University of Massachusetts Boston, a summer seminar for high school students representing all Boston neighborhoods.

Susanne Rubenstein teaches English at Wachusett Regional High School in Holden, Massachusetts. She is presently writing a book on publishing student writing.

Deborah Savarino is a special education teacher at Bedford High School. In addition to coaching teenagers to believe in their own ability to learn, solve problems, and find their own inner strengths, she is the mother of an inquisitive, joyful two year old.

Richard Schaye, a former Peace Corps volunteer in India, has served as a teacher and administrator in the Wayland Public Schools for nineteen years. He heads a task force on developing a model teacher training program to meet the needs of inner city students who are bused to suburban school districts in the Boston (MA) area.

Born in Mexico City, Sylvia B. Shaw is a Spanish teacher at Uxbridge High School. She lives happily in the woods by a lake with her husband and four children, publishes stories from time to time, and has had an on-going relationship with a novel for twenty-four years.

David Summergrad has taught at Wayland Middle School for twenty years. He has published several articles about middle school education, and he serves as a member of a local school board. He has been a presenter at the annual NCTE convention on the topic of heterogeneous grouping. He was recently honored as a recipient of the Distinguished Teacher Award.

Ruth E. Weiner has been an English teacher at Stoughton High School for the last fifteen years. She recently completed a master's degree in Computers in Education at Lesley College.

Anne Wheelock is the author of *Crossing the Tracks: How "Untracking" Can Save America's Schools* (New Press 1992).

# INDEX

Also available from Stenhouse...

# OOPS
*What We Learn When Our Teaching Fails*
Edited by Brenda Miller Power and Ruth Shagoury Hubbard

If every minute in your classroom is perfect, this book's not for you.

But if you've ever had a disaster as a teacher, then welcome to the world of *Oops* where things can—and *do*—go wrong. In these stories of failure—stories that will resonate with every teacher who took a risk and blew it—over 45 new and veteran teachers write about their mistakes and attempt to make sense of them.

There is sparkling humor and genuine pain in these stories of teachers who care deeply about their students and still make mistakes. Every failure matters, and often hurts. But ultimately, many teachers have learned the most about the art of teaching when their teaching fails.

1-57110-027-X                                                    Paperback

*For information on all Stenhouse publications,*
*please write or call for a catalogue.*

Stenhouse Publishers
P. O. Box 360
York, Maine 03909
(207) 363-9198